Emily Post

PROM AND PARTY ETIQUETTE

Emily Post

PROM AND PARTY ETIQUETTE

By Cindy Post Senning, Ed.D.,
and Peggy Post

Collins
An Imprint of HarperCollinsPublishers

Collins is an imprint of HarperCollins Publishers.

Prom and Party Etiquette
 For information address HarperCollins
Children's Books, a division of
HarperCollins Publishers, 10 East 53rd Street,
New York, NY 10022.
www.harpercollinschildrens.com

Library of Congress Cataloging-in-Publication Data
Senning, Cindy Post.
Prom and party etiquette / by Cindy Post Senning and Peggy Post.—1st ed.
p. cm.
ISBN 978-0-06-111713-8
1. Etiquette for children and teenagers. 2. Proms. 3. Parties.
I. Post, Peggy. II. Title. III. Title: Prom and party etiquette.
BJ1857.C5S39 2010 2009002795
395.3—dc22 CIP
AC

Typography by Jeanne L. Hogle
10 11 12 13 14 LP/RRDB 10 9 8 7 6 5 4 3 2 1
❖
First Edition

We dedicate this book to John and Allen,
with our gratitude for the happy times we've
shared with them. Thanks to both of you!
—C.P.S. and P.P.

ACKNOWLEDGMENTS

We acknowledge with deep appreciation the juniors and seniors from South Burlington High School, Burlington, Vermont, and Harwood Union High School in Duxbury, Vermont, who shared their stories, thoughts, and ideas about proms and other teen parties and then shared a pizza dinner with us as well!

We also want to thank the teens who responded to our online survey, helping us understand the ongoing importance these parties have for teens in every region of the country.

Peter Post from The Emily Post Institute and Katherine Cowles from the Cowles Agency provided invaluable assistance and creative advice, for which we are grateful.

And, finally, we want to say a special thank-you to Lizzie Post, also from The Emily Post Institute, for all her help with the research that formed the foundation for this book.

Thank you all!

CONTENTS

INTRODUCTION

ETIQUETTE: The Life of Every Party

For decades, teenagers just like you have celebrated their high school years at proms, homecomings, graduations, Valentine's Day dances, quinceañeras, sweet sixteens, and other parties. Over the years, these parties have been grounded in special traditions that have been handed down through generations. There are kings and queens, special themes and decorations, girls and boys in fancy formal wear, and that special someone to dance with.

Navigating all of these social events can be tricky. You may ask yourself: What should I wear? How can I be a good host or a model guest? Should I bring a gift? How much do I tip the limo driver? What's a boutonniere? The list is endless.

Relax. We're here to help. We can give you all the tools you need to get through all of these celebrations, using etiquette as our guide.

Etiquette dates back to the eighteenth century and comes from the French word for "ticket" or "little sign." All these years later, etiquette is still simply a collection of "little signs," or good manners, that can guide us in unfamiliar situations. Manners can help build good relationships and allow us to feel more comfortable everywhere.

All manners are rooted in just three principles:

1. Respect: caring for and understanding others just as they are—whether they come from different cultures or have different beliefs. Showing respect for others also sends a signal for others to respect you in return.
2. Consideration: thinking about how your actions will affect others around you.
3. Honesty: Honesty is more than just not telling lies. Honesty is about being sincere and direct in a way that produces positive results.

Etiquette is a combination of manners and these three principles. Both are critical, because manners can change over time and from place to place. For instance, a prom in South Carolina may be guided by different traditions and manners than a prom in Oregon. But both will be grounded in the principles of respect, consideration, and honesty.

Knowing some basic etiquette can help get you through all of the celebrations you may be invited to during your teen years. In this book we have shared basic manners that you can take to help you at the big dance—or anywhere. For each social event described in this book you will be faced with many choices—how to plan and what to do before, during, and after the party. There may not always be a right or wrong choice. When that is the case, our advice is to consult the three principles. You can never go wrong if you are respectful, considerate, and honest. Think through your choices, make your decision based on what is best for everyone, and, most of all, have a great time.

WHAT ETIQUETTE IS NOT

Etiquette is not about acting superior or wearing white gloves.

MAY
1 2 3 4 5 6
9 10 11 12

Chapter One

IT'S A PARTY!
What Do We Do Now?

You and your friends are sitting together at lunch. It's March and the dance is in two months. You're not even close to being ready. Who will you go with? What will you wear? How will you get there?

Don't worry. You still have time to plan, and in this chapter we'll cover everything you'll need to get started.

Your teen years will include a number of special parties: school dances, the prom, graduation, sweet sixteen, and quinceañera to name just a few. You may be the guest of honor, you may be in the prom court, or you may be one of many attendees. For each occasion you will be wondering about a date, invitation, clothes, flowers, gift, transportation, and food. While specific answers will depend on specific parties, we can supply general information that will fit any event. When you know what to expect—and what's expected of you—you can focus on having fun.

WHO?

Will I go with a date? Will I go with a group?

If you want to go to a party or a dance, the important thing is to find a way to make it possible.

Back in your grandmother's day, it would have been unthinkable for a girl to ask a boy out. She would have sat by her phone waiting, and waiting some more. And the boy might have been just as shy and was also sitting by his phone trying to get up his courage. And perhaps they both missed the dance. How sad! Today, it's perfectly acceptable for a girl to invite a

boy to a dance. Or a boy can ask a girl. A group of friends might decide to go together. A girl might go with her two best friends. The only limitations these days are those defined by the event. What a relief!

A QUESTION FOR CINDY AND PEGGY

QUESTION: ***There's this guy I've been hanging out with for the past month. He's supercute and really nice. We've gone to the movies, we text each other all the time, and we meet up for lunch almost every day. Next month is our school's annual winter ball. I think I want to ask him, but I'm scared. He hasn't asked me. We are not a "couple," and I don't want to make things awkward, but . . . what should I do?***

ANSWER: *You really should talk to this cute and oh-so-nice friend. Maybe he would love to go with you. Maybe he asked someone else before he even met you and doesn't know what to say. It's possible he doesn't like to dance and would rather not go at all. You'll only know if you ask. It would be a shame not to know what he really thinks. Go for it!*

Sometimes proms or dances are restricted to juniors and seniors. Some schools allow juniors and seniors to bring underclassmen. It may be the case that a tenth grader can go with a twelfth grader but not with a group of other tenth graders. Find out what the limitations are and then talk to your friends and figure out a plan.

If you are going to an event hosted in a private home, your invite might say "Plus One." If that's the case, then you can bring a date or a friend. If the invite does not specify, be sure to check in with your host before bringing an entourage.

THE DILEMMA

You've been asked to go to the prom with Elliot, the boy next door. You said yes. Now you've been asked to the prom by Roger, a very cute boy you did not imagine would ever ask you.

You would . . .

a. Thank Roger and tell him you already have a date.

b. Make up some lame excuse, tell Elliot that you have to break your date with him, and go with Roger.

c. Tell Elliot the truth (that you really want to go with Roger), break your date with him, and go with Roger.

Answers

a. This is the only *right* choice! In the long run, Roger and Elliot will have greater respect for you—and you will have greater respect for yourself—if you don't drop Elliot for Roger.

b. You will hurt Elliot, you will lose respect for yourself, and, if he finds out what happened, Roger will also lose respect for you.

c. It might work, but you are running the risk of hurting Elliot with the same results as in b.

Why risk it? You'll see Roger at the dance. And if he is half the guy you think he is, this won't be the only time he'll ask you out.

WHO PAYS?

Years ago it was assumed that guys paid for girls. The days of assuming are over. Nowadays it's acceptable for either the boy or the girl to pay or to split the cost. But there are many different scenarios. In one approach, the person who does the asking does the paying. If a girl buys two tickets to the dance and asks a boy, she would pay. If she buys the tickets, does she also buy dinner? Tradition would say "No! It is the boy who pays." However, a dinner at a fancy restaurant can be very expensive. Perhaps one of the couple pays for the tickets and one pays for the dinner.

Communication is the key in this situation. Maybe your date thinks tradition is the most important thing. Maybe you think both parties should contribute. If you talk it through and show respect for each other, you are sure to find an answer that works for both of you. The best bet is

to make decisions about financing the special event early enough so it doesn't become stressful. You do not want to get into a tug-of-war over the bill when the waiter brings it to the table.

$$$$—TRADITION VS. MODERN

The rules they are a-changing! The decision about who pays depends on which standard you apply:

1. **Tradition**—The boy pays for tickets, dinner, and limo or car. Each pays for the other's flowers.
2. **Modern**—The person who invites pays for tickets. The couple decides who will pay for dinner and limo or car.

Either one is okay and perfectly acceptable.

HOW DO I PLAN MY GUEST LIST?

There are many things to consider when planning your guest list:

- Do you ask everyone in your class or everyone in your building, only your "best" friends or everyone on your team?
- What if there is someone you don't especially like?
- What if you have eight good friends but can only invite six?

Whether you are planning a pre-prom dinner at your home or a post-graduation party at a local reception hall, deciding on the guest list is an important, challenging task. You want to get the right mix of people. Depending on the place you choose to host your gathering, you may be limited by space. The first question that must be addressed is, How many? There are three important considerations when you make this decision:

1. The *type* of party you are planning. A sit-down dinner may limit your numbers to six to ten. A buffet dinner may open up things and offer the opportunity for sixteen to twenty.
2. What is your *budget*? Can you afford four or fourteen?
3. *Space* is an important consideration. If you only have space for five, you can't invite fifteen.

The next question has to do with your relationships to the people involved. Are there two or three couples you know who are all good friends and would make things really fun? If it is your graduation party, do you need to invite family members? If your date is shy, it would be important to include some of his friends so he has someone he feels comfortable with.

Another question involves your knowledge about those you might invite. Do two of the people have a history of not getting along? Does everyone have a ticket to the dance you will all go to after the dinner at your home? If it is a graduation party, do some of your potential guests have their own obligations to family members?

After carefully considering all these questions, you are ready to build your list. Once you have all the names down on paper, take a look at the list as a whole. Picture guests on the evening of your event. Can you see them talking to one another, enjoying one another's company, and helping you to really celebrate and enjoy the special evening? After all, the guest list is really the heart of your party. Give it the attention it deserves.

HOW DO I ASK THEM?

Is the event a pre-prom, graduation, quinceañera, or sweet sixteen party? Is it casual or formal? Who's hosting it, you or your parents? How can your guests let you know if they can come or not? These are all essential pieces of information for the host and the guests. An invitation is like a road map. In just a few words, you can help your guests find their way to the party, literally and figuratively!

Whatever form your invitation takes, there are five pieces of essential information it should include:

1. *Who's hosting:* you, you and some friends, or your parents?
2. *What's the celebration:* coming-of-age, graduation, pre- or post-event party?
3. *When will it happen?* When you give the date, it also helps to indicate the day of the week and, of course, don't forget to mention the time. (If it's a pre-prom party, you might mention an end time so guests can plan rides to the prom.)
4. *Where will it be?* You can include directions or a small map if the place may not be familiar to everyone you invite.
5. *Any other information that your guests need to know:* Is it formal or casual; is there a theme; do you want the guests to bring something or not (add "No gifts, please" to your invitation if that is the case)?

RSVP (**R**épondez **S**'il **V**ous **P**laît, which means "Please respond" in French) on the invitation will let the guests know how to reply to your invite. It can be a huge help to know how many people are coming, especially if you are serving food and beverages. Some invitations say "Regrets only." That's just what they mean. If a person is planning to attend, he or she does NOT need to let the host know. Unless you really don't need to know how many are coming, you should indicate some form of reply on the invitation.

RSVP

Let your guests know the best way to reply to your invite!

By phone: RSVP to 809-555-8049 any evening.

By snail mail: RSVP to 320 Pollander Road, Berlin, MA 05525

By email: RSVP to Cyndi@myhouse.com

(If you still haven't heard from a guest within a week or two, it is completely okay to call or send an email to ask if he or she is planning to come.)

The style of your invitation tells your guests what type of party you are throwing.

A formal printed invitation with standard language signals to your guests that it's a formal event. For example, an invitation issued by your parents to your formal quinceañera could look like this:

MR. AND MRS. ROBERTO AGUILAR

REQUEST THE HONOR OF YOUR PRESENCE

AT A MASS CELEBRATING

THE FIFTEENTH BIRTHDAY

OF THEIR DAUGHTER

ROSA THERESA

ON SATURDAY, THE FOURTEENTH OF APRIL,

AT HALF PAST FOUR O'CLOCK

SAINT PETER'S ROMAN CATHOLIC CHURCH

ARLINGTON, MASSACHUSETTS

A reception card that offers the information for the party to follow is traditionally printed and included in the envelope.

PLEASE JOIN US AFTERWARD

FOR THE RECEPTION AT

THE ATLANTIC CLUB

808 SEASIDE AVENUE

ARLINGTON, MASSACHUSETTS

RSVP

2222 CONCORD AVENUE

LEXINGTON, MA 01002

A more casual, handwritten note can give the information needed but sends the message that your event is a smaller, intimate, and informal affair:

Dear Maggie,

I can't believe it! My sweet sixteen is coming up, and my parents are giving me a party. It will be at the beach club on Saturday, April 25, from 8:00 to 11:00. We're planning to barbecue on the beach, so save room for ribs. There will be a DJ and dancing. I hope everyone from our class will be there. If you want to bring a date that's totally fine, just please let me know ahead of time so we can keep track of the head count. You can give me a call at 555-8149 or send an email to me at Cyndi@myhouse.com.

Hope you can come,

Cyndi

A phone call is the most casual of all the invite options, but be sure to give your guest all the essential information. Sometimes on the phone you can get into a side discussion and perhaps forget to mention something important, like the time or date. It's a good idea to have all the information written down and in front of you as you make the calls, and go right down the list.

TIPS FOR PHONE INVITES

You can unintentionally put your friend on the spot if you say "What are you doing on Saturday?" or "Are you free on Saturday?"

It's better to give her the option to decide if it's the right event for her by saying "I'm having a dinner on Saturday before the prom. Can you and Jackson make it?"

An invitation by email is the newest form of a casual invitation. It has lots of advantages:

- Saves money on postage.
- Easy reply options for the guest.
- Speeds delivery.
- So many options for design.

There are also some disadvantages:

- It may get sent to someone's spam and you would never know. Then your guest wouldn't know either!
- Someone could forward it on to others without your knowledge.
- Some sites have a charge.
- You may send it to someone who doesn't check his or her email very frequently.

If you decide to go for it, search the internet for email invitations. You will find many sites with different options both in terms of content and ease of use. Pick an invitation style that suits you best and will get out all the information to your friends.

WHAT SHOULD I WEAR?

Whether the event is formal, casual, or somewhere in-between, you will want to look your best. A party offers a chance to step out a bit from everyday life. It usually marks a chance to create a special evening at every level. So think in terms of making yourself look special in whatever style fits the event.

Formal—What Does That Mean?

A specific style of dress is called for when the invitation or the ticket to the ball says the event is formal. When an event is formal, a certain tone of elegance is set, and people are supposed to dress in a similar manner. Formal means a black tuxedo, matching trousers, a white tuxedo shirt, and a bow tie for the guys and a formal evening

dress—a gown, a cocktail dress, or a dressy pants outfit—for the girls.

Semiformal—What Does That Mean?

The semiformal dress code lies somewhere between formal and casual. Traditionally, men wear dark, dressy business-type suits with or without a vest, a white shirt and a conservative tie, and dark shoes with dress socks. Most young men in high school don't have a lot of formal clothes, so the standard for "festive" attire may make more sense for a semiformal event. For festive attire, young men typically wear a seasonal sports coat or blazer and an open-collar shirt or a shirt with a colorful or holiday-theme tie. Sometimes guys don't have their own blazer, so they borrow from their fathers, older brothers, or friends.

Women are expected to wear a short afternoon or cocktail-style dress. Girls in high school are more likely than boys to have clothes that fit this standard. But they may also wear the more casual festive attire that adds dressy pants outfits to the mix.

Casual—What Does That Mean?

Just because an event is casual doesn't mean anything goes. You don't want to arrive at a friend's party (even if it is just for pizza!) looking like you came from the gym. Making yourself presentable shows the host that you respect the

BEYOND THE DRESS (OR JACKET)

Your overall appearance includes more than the dress or jacket you choose. Here are some other items to be mindful of:

- Cleanliness—Stains, dirt, and odors can spoil even the best look.
- Neatness—Show you care about yourself by looking wrinkle free and well put together.
- Hair care—Whatever the style, your hair should be clean; greasy looking or completely uncombed hair will make you look disheveled.
- Nail care—Make sure your nails are clean and well tended! (Girls: Bright colors and great designs can lose their impact if your nails are cracked or chipped, so take care of them until the evening is done!)
- Fresh breath—What's there to say? No one wants to be called out for bad breath. Fresh, minty breath takes only a little care with toothpaste, floss, and mouthwash.
- Jewelry and other accessories—Keep jewelry and other accessories simple and chic. You want them to accentuate, not dominate.
- Perfume and cologne—Sometimes less is more! A soft, subtle scent is perfect; a strong, overpowering scent does just that: It overpowers and actually can turn away some people.

All these elements are important in everyday dress as well as for the most formal event. In any case or any place, attention to these details will enhance your appearance and your enjoyment of the event at hand.

time she put into planning. So, for instance, jeans are a fine choice for a casual event, but you might take the chance to show off a new shirt or style your hair in a special way. Just remember: Casual does not mean compromising good taste!

Throughout your high school years there may be many opportunities to wear semiformal or festive attire. You may only need some accessories to look a little different or feel as if you have a "new" outfit for the event. For example, a basic black dress can be dressed up or down with scarves, jewelry, shoes, stockings, and/or a hairstyle. A blazer and slacks can look different with a different-color shirt or a special tie. If you decide to purchase an outfit that can be used in more than one setting, keep it simple so you can easily change it for any occasion.

Whether casual, formal, or in-between, your clothes should be clean, without holes or frayed edges, well fitting, and consistent with the type of event.

FLOWERS—A CORSAGE OR A BOUTONNIERE?

Think of flowers as a special gift for a special occasion. You want them to highlight the evening. Give your selection some thought. Ask your date about color and type. You don't want the corsage or boutonniere to clash with what you are wearing. If your date asks you about colors, give him or her a few options. If you limit your choice to just one, your date may have difficulty finding what you want.

Beyond colors there will be a choice of style. For a woman, a corsage can be pinned near the shoulder, at the waist, or to her bag or clutch. If pinned to the shoulder, the flowers should face up. If pinned at the waist, position it in the most attractive manner. Many florists will suggest a wristlet. This is a corsage with an elastic band and can be worn on a woman's wrist like a bracelet. This is popular, as it doesn't get crushed when the woman is dancing. A wristlet can easily become a corsage: The elastic band can be clipped off and the flowers pinned on.

A girl may give her date a boutonniere: a single flower that is pinned to the lapel of the jacket right where the buttonhole would be. The most common flowers used in a boutonniere are a rose or a carnation. The choice may be determined by your budget: roses tend to be more expensive. You can choose a color with the help of your florist—there is no standard that determines the color. The boutonniere will come with a straight pin that can be thread over and under the lapel fabric to secure the flower in place.

TO "GIFT" OR NOT

Whether or not to give a gift depends on the occasion. Typically, other than a corsage or boutonniere, you do not give a gift when going to a party that is for everyone, such as a dance at school or a prom. On the other hand, a coming-of-age party—such as a quinceañera, a bar or bat mitzvah, or a sweet sixteen—and a party to celebrate an accomplishment—such as a graduation—often carry the expectation of a gift. Check with the host if you are unsure about gift giving.

NO GIFT?

The person giving the party may choose to say "No gifts," in which case it is important to go along with that request. If you want to give a birthday or graduation present to the guest of honor, you certainly may—just do it at some other time!

Gifts may or may not be opened at the event. Sometimes it is simpler to wait until afterward. That way, if someone did not bring a gift, he or she won't be embarrassed. Also, there is less chance for comparisons being made between gifts; and if there are duplicate gifts, the giver or recipient won't be as apt to feel bad. If gifts are opened, make it a part of the event. Once people have their beverages, everyone can sit around the guest of honor, who can open gifts and give each one the appropriate attention it deserves. This allows the gift opener to thank each attendee personally right then and there. The in-person, face-to-face thank-you is the nicest one of all, and opening gifts at the party will give you a chance to do just that.

A QUESTION FOR CINDY AND PEGGY

QUESTION: ***At my graduation I opened the gifts and personally thanked everyone as I opened his or her gift. Do I need to send a thank-you note also?***

ANSWER: *If you have said thank you face-to-face and you have been able to show your appreciation to the giver, that is the nicest thanks of all and you are "technically" not required to send a note as well. However, it never hurts. It is so easy to miss thanking someone at a busy party or to have a quick thank-you get lost in the festivities. Sending a note ensures that your appreciation is expressed and heard.*

SPEAKING OF THANK-YOU

You can show your appreciation by thanking people for gifts of time and energy as well as material gifts. Consider a special thank-you in person or in a note to:

Whoever hosted your party: your parents, a neighbor, or a close relative. It takes an amazing amount of work to plan and host a party. Taking the time to write a note, make a call, or seek out your host for a personal thank-you is the very least you can do.

The committee members who planned the prom or school dance. They have worked for hours on your behalf. A simple thank-you can mean so much to someone who has devoted so much time to the event you had the opportunity to enjoy.

The chaperones who volunteered to be at your school dance. They spent an evening helping you and your classmates have a special party. They were there to greet you; they kept watch on the sidelines; they were on hand to help if problems arose; they made sure everyone had safe transportation home and no one was left behind or alone at the school. A personal or written thank-you may mean they will be willing to help out again so future students can enjoy their special event.

A GOOD HOST, A GOOD GUEST, A GOOD ATTENDEE

Whatever the occasion, whatever the party, its success depends on the people there. The decorations can fall down, the food can be spilled, the music can be unexpected; but if the hosts and the guests have a good spirit and bring joy and fun to the event, it can be memorable in every way.

A Good Host

The primary focus of a great host must be his or her guests. If everyone feels welcome, has a good time, and leaves knowing he or she would want to return to another party given by the host, then the host has done the job well. So, what can a host do to make sure everyone is comfortable and has a good time? A good host:

- Lets everyone know all the information he or she will need: time, place, directions, what to wear, what food will be served, what to bring (if anything), and whether or not to RSVP.
- Gives himself plenty of time to prepare everything that can be prepared in advance: dinner, beverages, or snacks.
- Gives herself plenty of time to set up things: chairs and tables, the table setting, place cards (if the choice is to assign seating), decorations, and general cleanup.
- Makes himself available to greet guests when they arrive.
- Watches throughout the party for the guest who is left alone or seems to be on the sideline.
- Offers food and beverages to everyone throughout the party.

- Talks to everyone.
- Makes herself available to say good-bye and thank you as each guest leaves.

The success of any great party is determined in large part by the host. If the host is so engrossed in putting on the party that he or she is stressed and working the whole time, then the party is probably not going to be a success. So when you are the host, plan ahead and leave yourself time to enjoy your own party, and you will host an event that ends with everyone, including you, having had a memorable time!

A Good Guest

No matter how much planning, how much food, how great the music, or how great the host, if the guests mope around or hang out in cliques and exclude others, everyone will be relieved when the party is over. That is not the outcome for which you are hoping. There are many things the guest can do to help create a festive and fun atmosphere. A good guest:

- Arrives on time or within fifteen minutes of the time on the invitation.
- Greets the host (if the host is not near the door, find him or her).
- Mingles, talks to all the guests.

- Tries different foods.
- Doesn't deviate from the host's plans (if there is a seating arrangement, honor the host's placements and don't rearrange the settings).
- Offers to help out, especially if the host is looking overwhelmed.
- Takes care of the host's things.
- Does not settle in to watch a favorite television show.
- Seeks out the host to say good-bye and thank you when leaving.
- SMILES!

When you accept an invitation, you do have a responsibility to make an effort to contribute to the party in a positive way. Maybe you've had a bad day or you might be feeling tired and out of sorts, but you can make the choice to set that behind you and enjoy the event. If you visit all your troubles on the other guests, your troubles won't go away.

All you will do is set up things so the others may join you in your misery. That is not very fair to the host or anyone else. On the other hand, if you show up with a positive attitude, a sense of fun, and a smile, you will make others feel that way also, and the party will be a success.

A Good Attendee

At some parties you are neither the guest nor the host. When you go to the school homecoming dance or the prom, you are one among many attendees. There is a slightly different list of behaviors that will help make the dance a success. A good attendee:

- Waits patiently if there is a line for signing in or giving tickets to a chaperone or committee member.
- Makes an effort to greet others even if they are not in your particular group. Just a smile and a "Hi" are enough.
- Follows the guidelines that are part of the deal: stays in the area designated, doesn't leave and return, doesn't smoke, doesn't bring his or her own food, or whatever else has been agreed to by purchasing a ticket for the event.
- Doesn't do anything that he might feel embarrassed about the next day.

- Uses basic social manners if snacks are served:
  - Doesn't talk with a mouth full of food.
  - Doesn't double-dip chips but instead spoons a small amount of dip on an individual plate.
  - Is careful when putting a drink down so it won't easily be spilled.
  - Takes a manageable amount of food on an individual plate and goes back for more if necessary. (Avoid piling your plate high with food as if you haven't had anything to eat in weeks.)
- Wears formal clothes to formal affairs; dresses casually for informal events.
- Shows respect when slow dancing. (Holding hands, putting arms around each other, or giving a light, quick kiss during a slow dance is fine; but a dance is not the place for heavy petting or passionate kissing and embraces!)
- Avoids loud, raucous behavior that interferes with anyone else's evening.
- Says good night and thank you to the chaperones and committee members she knows personally when the party's over.

THREE IN ONE

There may actually be a time when you can be a host, a guest, and an attendee all in one night.

1. You host a pre-prom dinner for eight at your house.
2. You go to the senior prom at the local banquet hall.
3. You are a guest at your good friend's post-prom party.

At each of these parties, as long as you act in ways that are respectful and considerate of the others, it doesn't matter whether you are the guest or the host. The main thing is to have a good time and help those around you to have a good time also!

It's all a matter of choice. You can have a positive impact on someone else's evening. Others have spent hard-earned money to be there, they have looked forward to it for months, and everyone acknowledges that there are not many opportunities for these parties. Choose to be more than a good attendee—be a great one. You have the power!

CHAPTER TWO

FROM BARBECUE TO BANQUET HALL: Party Food

A prom, a graduation party, a quinceañera, a winter ball, a sweet sixteen party, or a Valentine's Day dance: What do they have in common? At all of these parties you can be sure there will be food. Food might be served in a variety of ways: as a buffet, a sit-down dinner, or finger food and munchies.

Picture this: There is a banquet-style dinner at the Valentine's Day dance at your school. The girl sitting across from you is wearing a beautiful gown. Her hair looks terrific! Her nails are impeccable. And then . . . she starts talking and eating at the same time! You can actually see the chewed food in her mouth. So gross! She spent money and time to get just the right look and then . . . what else is there to say?

Table manners are not just silly rules made up to make our lives difficult. Table manners have evolved to accomplish two important things: They help minimize the potential grossness of eating, and they let you know what's expected so you can approach every meal with confidence. Here are some essential table manners to follow at every meal:

1. Wash your hands before coming to the table. It is unappetizing for everyone else at the table to see you picking up your food or utensils with dirty hands, not to mention unhealthy for you.
2. Put your napkin in your lap as soon as you are seated.
3. Wait until everyone is served before you start eating.
4. Locate and use the proper utensils. Your fork will always be on the left side of your plate. Knowing this will prevent you from using your neighbor's fork by mistake.
5. If soup is served, use your spoon and scoop away from your body or tip the bowl away to get that last drop. If you scoop or tilt toward your body, you run the risk of spilling the soup on your lap.
6. Pass dishes to the right.
7. Always chew with your mouth closed. Wait until

you have swallowed to speak.

8. Cut your food into manageable, bite-sized pieces so you don't overfill your mouth. Large bites are hard to swallow!
9. Break a bite-sized piece off your slice of bread, butter it, and then eat it rather than butter the whole slice of bread, and bite off a piece. This way you won't get butter all over your hands!
10. Use your napkin to wipe your face if you get sauce on your chin or milk on your upper lip.
11. Keep elbows (and other body parts!) off the table while eating.
12. Don't make bad comments about the food.
13. Say "Please pass the . . ." instead of reaching.
14. Don't make rude noises such as burping or slurping.
15. Remain at the table until everyone is done eating.
16. Thank your host or whoever prepared the meal.

No one expects you to be a fine-dining expert, but if you follow these essential guidelines you'll be just fine—whether it's at home, in a restaurant, or at a banquet.

If you don't know what to do, here's an easy tip: Just wait and watch what others do. If the food is unusual and you're not sure how to eat it or if you don't know which utensil to use, watch your host and then follow his example.

It may take some practice, but after a while these skills will become a habit and you won't even have to think about them. A great soccer player doesn't think about her skills; a great dinner companion doesn't think about his skills, either. Now you'll be ready to eat with confidence at any party and make a great impression. One more thing . . .

The Right Tools

Many people are surprised at the extent to which they are judged on the way they handle their utensils. Forks, spoons, and knives are tools for eating. As with any tools, they are most efficient when used correctly in every sense. You wouldn't want to hold a saw the wrong way. Why would you hold your fork the wrong way?

When using your fork, think about how you hold a pencil. The correct way to hold a fork is essentially the same. Grasp the fork between your thumb and index finger about midway down the handle and rest and steady the handle on your third finger just under where you are holding it. Your fourth and fifth fingers simply support your third finger. It's really quite simple.

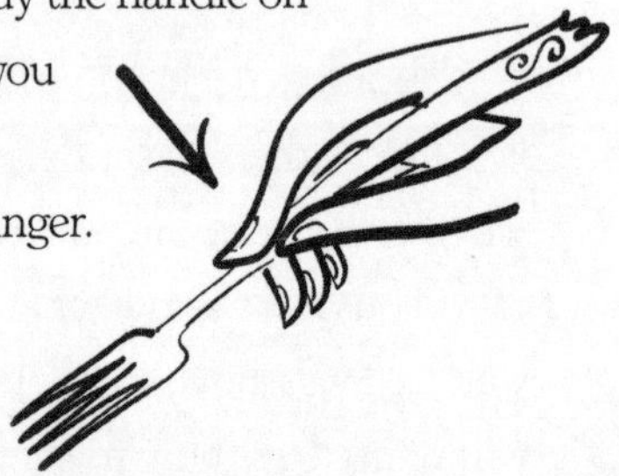

If you hold your fork and knife pointing down into

THERE ARE TWO STYLES FOR EATING AND BOTH ARE OKAY

American (or zigzag) style. After the food is cut, the American method calls for you to place the knife on the edge of the plate. Then you switch the fork to your right hand, slide it under the bite of food you want, and raise it *tines up* to your mouth.

Continental style. Once the food is cut, you either keep the knife in your hand or lay it across the plate as you lift the fork with the bite on it to your mouth. The knife and fork stay in the same hands you used while you were cutting. The fork is held tines down with the index finger touching the neck of the handle.

your meat like spears, you are likely to slide that meat off the side of your plate because you really have very little control of it. Instead, if you hold the fork and knife "correctly," you have complete control. Give it a try:

Hold your knife in your right hand (reverse this if you're left-handed) with your index finger pressed just below where the handle meets the blade. Hold the fork tines (points) down in your left hand and spear the food to steady it, pressing the base of the handle with your index finger. As you cut your food, keep your elbows at table height—

not raised high or pointed straight out.

If you have not been holding your fork and knife this way up until now, it will feel awkward at first; but with practice it will get easier. Don't give up!

TEEN PARTIES AND FOOD—FROM FORMAL DINNER TO SNACKS

There are basically four possible eating experiences associated with teen parties that you may encounter. All the manners related to food and eating are applicable no matter what the setting. But for each setting you may encounter specific situations that require a slightly different or special manner.

Restaurant dining: You may spring for a nice dinner at a local restaurant on prom night. This may be the first time you've been out to a fancy dinner on your own with your classmates, so you'll want to make sure everything goes smoothly. Here are some basic tips:

- Make a reservation—whether it is simply the two of you on a date or a group of six or eight, call ahead and make a reservation. This is especially important on prom night, because restaurants fill up quickly. When you call, be prepared to give a specific number of diners and the time you plan to arrive. Be ready with a second-choice restaurant just in case the first is already booked.

- Plan how you will pay the bill before the event. Check ahead of time to see if you can get separate checks and pay with a credit card if necessary. Some restaurants are cash only, so you don't want to get caught with empty pockets!
- If you are getting separate checks but some couples will be paying together, they should order together also. This makes it easier for the waiter to keep track of the billing.
- Arrive five minutes before the reservation time to ensure that you don't lose your table. Use this time to put away your coats and get your party together before you are seated.
- Thank the maître d' or whoever takes you to the table.
- People go to an elegant restaurant to enjoy a special meal. Be considerate of other diners by speaking at a normal volume. Avoid loud and raucous behavior.
- If there is a problem with your meal (it's cold or it's not what you ordered), gesture to your waiter to come over and then quietly tell him what the problem is. If you simply don't care for what you ordered, there is nothing you can do.
- When you are finished, place your fork and knife

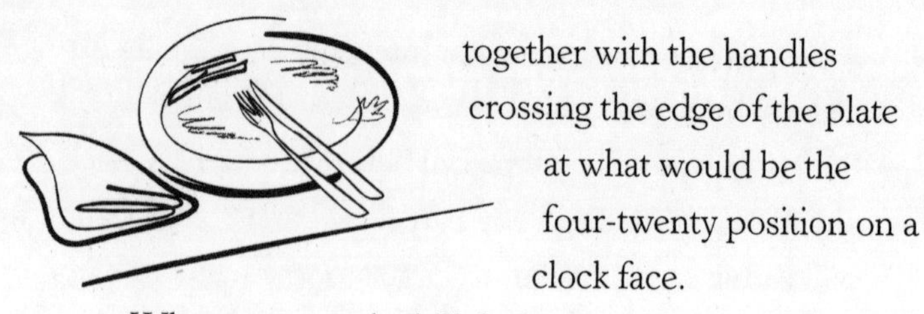

together with the handles crossing the edge of the plate at what would be the four-twenty position on a clock face.

- When you pay the bill, be sure to tip the waiter 20 percent. Tipping the wait staff is an important courtesy. It can be paid on a credit card or in cash. If you pay the tip in cash, leave the money inside the small bound folder that restaurants typically use to bring the bill to the table. If you pay the tip on a credit card, do not forget to write the amount on the slip and add it into your total. If there is a coatroom attendant, tip him or her one dollar per coat.

Dinner at a restaurant can be pricey, so be prepared. If it is your choice to add this special meal to your prom night, be sure to include it in your budget. Many restaurants post their menus and prices online, and you can use that as a guide. If the menu isn't posted, visit the restaurant and look at the menu in person.

Dinner at home: Maybe there is no room at the restaurant. Maybe it's too expensive. Or perhaps you want to be a little more relaxed. There are many reasons not to eat out before the dance. Dinner at home can be just as enjoyable. It doesn't have to be a five-course meal. After all,

WHERE TO PUT THAT NAPKIN

- When you first sit down at the table, place the napkin in your lap.
- If you leave to go to the restroom or when you leave at the end of the meal, put the napkin on the table beside your plate.

In either case, if there is a greasy or messy spot on your napkin, fold that spot under a cleaner section so the other diners don't have to look at it while they are still eating or, if it's the end of the meal, the waiters don't have to worry about getting it on their hands.

Special note: Do not put your napkin on the seat of your chair. If there is food on it, the food can get on the chair. If the chair has a cloth seat, the fabric can get stained or ruined by a dirty napkin. There is always the chance that when you return, you pick up your napkin, sit on the food, and stain your beautiful gown.

you want to spend your time preparing for the dance, not preparing a fancy dinner. There are a couple of options:

1. Keep the dinner simple—something you can prepare ahead of time and heat just before it's time to eat.
2. Order takeout. You can set the table with a tablecloth, your family's nicest plates, candles, flowers, and pretty napkins (paper or cloth). Replace the plastic containers for the take-out food with dishes. This will make the table more attractive. Enjoy being with your guests instead of cooking.

If you decide to host friends in your home, review the section on hosting from Chapter One (pages 26–27). If the whole group is headed to the dance after your dinner, be sure that everyone has a ride.

A banquet at the dance or at a banquet hall: At some school dances the price of the ticket includes a dinner. Everyone who goes has dinner together in a big hall or, if the dance is at the school, the cafeteria. Usually the planning committee has arranged for decorations that really transform the room.

If the committee has arranged to have the school kitchen staff, a caterer, or a local restaurant prepare the meal, it may actually be served as a sit-down dinner. In that case, everyone is served the same thing. (There may be choices

A PARENTS' GIFT

We've heard stories about parents who chose to prepare dinner as a gift to their party-going son or daughter. One story was about three sets of parents who organized, prepared, and served a meal for eighteen kids. They set up three tables with six settings each in a basement family room. They decorated the room, set up special lighting, made the tables look elegant, and did the cleanup after the kids left for the dance. The teens will remember the dinner as a demonstration of care and respect that the parents showed for them, and the parents will remember the dinner as a way they shared the special evening with their children.

offered when you buy the ticket, such as a chicken, fish, or vegetarian entrée.) The diners can make it easier for the servers by moving aside a little as plates are served and keeping their hands in their laps. This is one time you do not offer to help clear. Let the servers do that. In fact, unless the server asks for help, the diners shouldn't stack or pick up plates for removal.

Other banquet dinners may be served as buffets. Here are some basic manners for buffets:

- You can walk along the table to see what's there before getting in line.
- Wait patiently in line.
- Don't cut the line.
- If it is serve-yourself style, take moderate helpings. The point of a buffet is that you can return as often as you please, so you don't have to overload on the first trip.
- If there is someone serving the dishes, be sure to say "Thanks!"

WHOSE IS WHOSE?

At any sit-down affair—whether it's at a restaurant, a private home, or a banquet hall—there is the possibility that the table will be crowded with dishes, napkins, utensils, glasses, cups, and saucers. How do you know which items are yours? That's what table settings are all about.

The basics: When you sit at the table, your plate is the one directly in front of you. Your napkin is either on your plate or to the left of it. Your forks are the ones on your left, your knife is on your right, and your spoon is to the right of your

B AND *D*

A frequently asked question: Which one is my bread plate? I can never remember, and I don't want to eat someone else's roll.

A trick: Hold your hands out in front of you, palm facing palm about six inches apart. Bring the tips of your thumb and index fingers together to form a circle on each hand. Raise your middle, ring, and pinky fingers straight up behind the circle in an "okay" sign. Look at each hand. Your left hand should look like a small letter *b,* as in *bread.* If you're sitting in front of a place setting, your fingers are pointing to your *b*read plate. Your right hand should look like a small *d,* as in *drink*. Your right fingers are pointing to your *d*rink.

At the table, simply put your hands in your lap and make the "okay" signs, and your fingers will be pointing to *your* bread plate and *your* drinks.

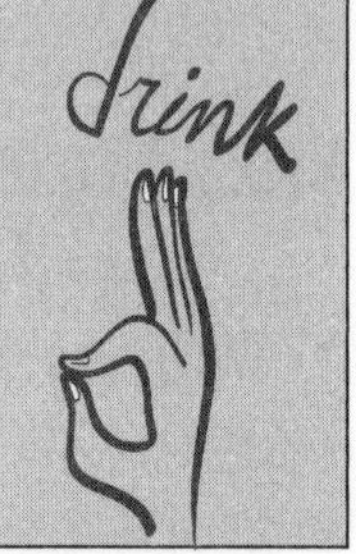

knife. Your salad (if it is set out when you sit down) is either on a salad plate in front of you or to the left of your forks. Your bread and butter plate is on the left above your forks, and your glass(es) are on the right above your knife and spoon. Your cup and saucer is the set on your right, next to the spoon.

Chips, Dips, and Veggies Table

Not all dances and parties have a meal associated with them. Usually, though, the hosts will want to serve some form of beverage or snack. Whether at home, school, or a banquet hall, you are likely to see a long table against one wall with a variety of snacks on it. Chips and dips of all sorts, veggies (carrots, celery, summer squash, cherry tomatoes), tiny sandwiches, and cheese and crackers are the most common. At both ends of the table there is usually a stack of small plates and napkins.

Some basic manners for the snack table include:

- Take a plate and napkin and pass along in front of the table.
- Take a small amount of the things that look good to you.
- Try not to pile your plate too high. This is just a snack table. It is not intended to be your dinner for the evening.

- Spoon some of the dip you want onto your small plate.
- Don't eat while in line.
- Hold the napkin under the plate or between the fourth and fifth fingers and the palm of your hand.

DON'T DOUBLE-DIP!

Question: If I have a huge chip, scoop it in the dip, and take a bite, can I scoop it in the dip again?

Answer: In a word, don't. That is called double-dipping, and it is not okay—unless, of course, the dip is on your own little personal plate. The idea is that you should not scoop in a common bowl with a chip after you've put the chip in your mouth.

IN EVERY SITUATION

Whether you are eating cheese and crackers at the snack table or sitting at a formal table in a restaurant, it is important to remember that the reason you are there is social. It is even more important than eating. You want your date and your friends to be comfortable and to enjoy the event as much as you do. These eight tips will help you keep things fun and sociable:

1. If you're sitting at a table, talk to people on both sides of you.
2. If you're standing in a group, include everyone in your conversation.
3. Don't whisper.
4. Don't be loud and dominate the conversation.

5. Avoid controversial topics that have the possibility of ending in an argument.
6. Avoid personal topics that may cause an emotional reaction.
7. Don't interrupt.
8. Listen!

Chapter Three

PROM NIGHT: Kings, Queens, and Special Themes

One of the most special events of the year is the prom. Sometime in May, high school juniors and seniors get together in the school gym, a local banquet hall, or a nearby hotel for an evening of music, dance, food, and fun with friends. Teens across the country anticipate, enjoy, and remember this special event for years to come. Every prom has a unique combination of local traditions and those that are shared by high school teens across the country:

- Formal dress—tuxedos and gowns
- Music and dance
- Beautiful decorations—often with a theme
- Guests might be seniors only, maybe juniors only, maybe juniors and seniors together; or perhaps freshmen and sophomores are allowed as dates

- A king, queen, and royal court
- A red-carpet entrance
- Food at the prom OR special dinner arrangements before the prom

The traditions guide the event. Etiquette provides the tools you need to navigate the traditions and enjoy the prom.

Plan Ahead

Half the fun of the prom is the anticipation. There are so many exciting things to plan, but allow yourself enough time to prepare. Start your planning early so you don't miss something that is of special importance to you or your date. So, the first thing to settle on is who you'll be going with: a special date, a friend, or a group of friends (see Chapter One, page 6). Once that's taken care of, you can do your planning with the person (or people) with whom you're going. When the tickets for the prom go on sale, you know that it's time to start your planning.

GETTING TO THE PROM?

Limousine

You're dressed in a long ball gown; your date looks oh-so-dashing in his tuxedo. A long, white, shiny limousine pulls up to the door. An elderly man in a chauffeur's outfit

steps out and opens the door for you. You *know* that you are a princess! This has to be the most elegant thing you've ever done. For many teens, renting a limo to go to the prom is an essential part of the whole event. If, indeed, that is your choice, it will require some planning:

- How much will it cost?
- Will you have help paying for it: parents? date? others in the limo?
- Who will join you in the limo? It may be just you and your date; or a stretch limo if you are going in a group of six or eight.
- Will it pick each of you up at a different location, or will you all gather in one spot for the pickup?
- Who will make the reservation?
- Will you hire it to get to the prom, to get back home,

or both? If it's both, will the limo wait at the event? If you hire a limo only to get to the prom, how will you get home?

- Do you care if the limo's white or black? Do you have a choice?

The more answers you have, the better you will be able to plan. Since most teens attending the prom will be making their arrangements to get there, you don't want to wait until the last minute to line up others to join you in the limo. Plan ahead!

Car

Sure, a limo would be great, but there's nothing wrong with the family car. In fact, most teens go to the prom either in the family car or in a friend's car. The next important question is, Who will be driving? Here are some items

TIP THE DRIVER

Two questions:

1. **Do you tip the driver?** Yes, but most limousine companies automatically add a gratuity to the bill, so you do not have to worry about tipping the driver as you get out of the car.
2. **How much should you tip the driver?** If it is not included in the bill, you should be prepared to tip the driver 20 percent of the bill.

to consider when using a personal car.

- Clean it out! You or your date may have spent hundreds of dollars on clothes. The last thing either of you wants to do is enter a dirty or messy car.
- Plan who will be going! If there is only space for four, the third couple in your group may need to plan something different. Be clear about the plan so your good friend isn't scrambling for a ride at the last minute.
- Gas up! Maybe everyone can chip in, but do fill up one way or another. What a shame it would be to miss the prom because you're standing by the side of the road trying to hitch a ride to the nearest gas station.

BE RESPONSIBLE, STAY SAFE

While alcohol is not served at any prom, there may be alcohol at after-prom parties. If you agree to drive, you also agree to be the designated driver—meaning you agree to stay sober! If the driver does end up drinking, it is not only your choice, it is your obligation to find another way home and to help prevent others from getting in the car with someone who's been drinking.

If you don't have a license or a car available, planning for a ride is crucial! Don't make the mistake of *assuming* you can ride with a friend. Be clear about the plan so you are assured a seat in the car both for you and for your date. If your friends' cars are full, you may need to ask a parent or older sibling to drive.

Picture this: The day of the prom, you notice that your sister, who has agreed to drive you and your date to the prom and to pick you up later, is packing her overnight bag. When you remind her that it's prom night, she gasps and says, "Oh no . . . I completely forgot! I made other plans to visit Maria for the night. I'm so sorry! I guess I can't give you a ride."

Whatever your plan, double-check it a few days before the prom. What is an important, unforgettable date etched in your brain may not be so for your older sister. Remind her that she's agreed to give you a lift several days ahead so she keeps the evening available. Otherwise you may be spending the afternoon finding transportation when you had planned to be getting ready.

GOWNS AND TUXEDOS

Proms are traditionally formal affairs. (see Chapter One, page 18). It's part of the fun of the event and one of the elements that makes the night so special. You can wear your jeans every day, but how often do you get to dress up in a gown or a tuxedo?

Buying a Gown

One key to finding a great gown is to start early! You

can check out the shops in your hometown. For a wider selection, you might consider taking a trip to a nearby city. Make it a fun, full-day event: grab your mom, your sister, or some friends for fashion advice; go to the big department stores; search out smaller dress shops; have a nice lunch; and maybe even search for matching shoes if you have time. Or you can order a gown online. You will find many sites that feature gowns in every style, color, and price range.

KEEPING ON BUDGET

Let's face it: A prom can get pretty pricey for girls. Between the dress, the shoes, the jewelry, the hair, the makeup, and the purse, it's easy to see how people can get carried away. It's wise to consider a budget that you can afford before you go shopping. It's easy to get caught up in the moment and spend more than you should. But you'll regret it later when you're scrimping for weeks to make up for it. A beautiful look can be assembled on any budget. You don't have to shell out to be a knockout.

Here are some tips for keeping down the cost of your prom ensemble:

1. **Borrow, borrow, borrow!** Borrowing should be done carefully. Just be sure that you can replace the item you borrow if it is lost or ruined. With that one warning in mind, borrowing can be the easiest way to pull together an outfit on a budget—whether it's your whole look or maybe just a great pair of earrings.
2. **What's most important to you?** If the gown is the absolute most important thing for you, spend your money on your dress. Then you can choose to go to discount stores or borrow from friends for your shoes and accessories.
3. **DIY (Do It Yourself)!** You can find ways to get the look you want at home. For example, fashion magazines are always running features on new hairstyles and how to create them on your own, so grab a few magazines and start looking for ideas. Practice creating the style you want at least once before the big day. By doing a trial run you can see if you actually like the style and also make sure that you and your "stylist" (aka your bff, your mom, or your cool aunt Angela) know how to create the look you want.

4. This goes for makeup, too. Find styles you like and practice applying them so that you'll get it right on prom night.

Here are some things to consider as you look for your gown:

- **Color**—This is not the evening to experiment with a color you've never worn. In the store it may look great, but if you get home and are wondering what ever made you choose that color, it can be a lasting disappointment—and an expensive one at that.
- **Style**—A long, clingy dress may be flattering; but if you want to get out on the dance floor, you may find that it restricts your movements. The same advice goes for styles that are low cut: You don't want to spend the whole evening worried that your breasts will pop out!
- **Fabric**—Choose a fabric that drapes well, moves well, and flatters your body. Avoid garments that are made of very thin or sheer material, which will show every line and crease. You may need to select undergarments that work with the cut and style of your dress.
- **Fit**—Buy something that fits. Don't buy a gown for the body you hope to have in six weeks. Love the body you have now and buy a dress for that

body. Use the salespeople in the store to help if you are unsure about the fit. If you find that you are in between sizes, buy the larger one and have it tailored to fit.

- **Shoes**—To coordinate your shoes with your gown, opt for a neutral shoe color such as black or tan. Finding a shoe color that matches the shade of your dress is also an option but can be a bit harder. Some stores can dye shoes to match the color of your dress if that's in your budget. Finding the right fit is also important. If your shoes are too small, you can spend your evening in pain. If you buy new shoes for the event, wear them around the house for a few days to break them in. Pack a few bandages in your purse just in case the shoes rub or blister your feet.

Renting a Tuxedo

Once you're sure you are going to the prom and you know you'll be wearing a tux, don't wait too long to lay your hands on one. All the other guys in your class will be looking to rent or buy one, too. There are more options than you might realize; and the sooner you go, the more options you will have. Will you wear a cummerbund or suspenders? Will your shirt have a ruffled front? Will your shirt have studs or buttons? Some tuxedos have a stripe down the pant leg; some trousers are plain. There may be a vest under the jacket. There are many ways to go; the choice is yours.

Renting a tuxedo may not cost as much as buying a gown, but it can be expensive. The range can be significant, so shop around. Then be prepared for some hidden costs:

- You may need a deposit, so be prepared.
- Each extra will add cost. The more basic you go, the less expensive it will be. Don't worry, even the most basic tuxedo looks elegant!
- A sample of extras:
  - Cummerbund or vest
  - Bow tie
  - Ruffle-trimmed shirt (rather than plain front)
  - Cuff links
  - Studs (instead of buttons)
  - Dress socks
- Most shops will want you to return the tuxedo within a specified time. It may cost you extra if you bring it back late, so plan ahead.

THE TUXEDO—WHERE ON EARTH DID IT COME FROM?

Where did the craze start? Who created this getup, and why do we still wear it to formal events?

Tuxedos undoubtedly got their name from Tuxedo Park, the first planned residential community in New York. Emily Post's father was the architect, and she actually grew up spending her summers at Tuxedo Park.

One evening, Griswold Lorillard, son of the founder of Tuxedo Park, came up with the idea to wear a short black jacket without tails. The new fashion was a hit. When male guests would come and stay with families in Tuxedo Park, they were intrigued by the jackets the men wore and would return to places such as New York City and ask their tailors to make them a jacket "like the ones worn in Tuxedo." Ironically, the tuxedo was originally considered an informal dinner jacket (because of its short tails), and yet now it is the most formal attire for men to wear.

- How about shoes? Your hiking boots or sneakers will not work with your tuxedo (although there is the story of a young man who wore his purple high-tops with his tuxedo just to make a statement; everyone loved them!). Some shops rent shoes as well as tuxes. Again, the sooner you go to the shop to reserve your tux, the more choices you will have.

A Matching Look

Picture this: You've just rented your tuxedo. The clerk brings out this magnificent cummerbund and bow tie.

They are a great shade of red, and you know they will look amazing. You get to your date's house, she walks down the stairs, and you both realize at the same time that your red cummerbund and tie clash completely with her orange gown. Many teens avoid this scenario by talking ahead of time. Sometimes the girl may even give the guy a swatch of material. That way he can match his accessories to her whole look.

And it's not just a matter of color. Talk with your date about style—especially if you want to do something crazy. Some guys like to have fun with their look and go a little over the top. A boy might choose a ruffled shirt or calf-length pants with high stockings and buckled shoes. However, maybe his date is planning to wear a modern-looking gown with matching heels. The clash of styles might not be what either had in mind. All it takes is communication. The teens that we polled confirmed that dressing for the prom is a significant aspect of the whole affair, and taking the time to talk with your date assures a match in more ways than one.

Hair!

Ladies, a fancy gown deserves a fancy hairstyle. How will you do your hair? Will you do it yourself? Will your mother or your sister help you? Will you go to a hairdresser? Spend some time with a fashion magazine. Pick out styles that you think you would like and that are possible with your hair type.

If you plan to color, curl, or straighten your hair, it is a good idea to try these things out ahead of time. Use a color rinse to see how you really look with jet-black hair if that's your plan. Curl your hair in the style you envision so you can decide if it really suits the shape of your face. If you decide to go the hairdresser route, reserve your time slot early. There may be other girls with the same plan. How disappointing if you have your heart set on a fancy hairstyle you could never do on your own only to discover that all the hairdressers in town are booked that day!

Gentleman, whether you have long or short hair, you still want to ensure it is neat and clean for the big night. This may involve getting a trim at the barbershop or simply brushing and tying your long hair back into a ponytail. Try some different looks and styles. You may not have time the evening of the prom for a cut or trim, so play it safe and do it a few days beforehand.

BEFORE THE PROM . . .

Dinner or Not?

In Chapter Two you can review the options available to help you with your dining decisions. They are all acceptable, and each couple going to the prom must decide which works the best for them.

The really important thing is to plan for **something**. With all the excitement and activities, you need to remember to eat. You definitely don't want your stomach growling in the middle of that romantic slow dance!

Photo Ops

You may only go to one prom in your life. Even if you go to two or three, a prom is still a special occasion. Photos are an important part of capturing this special event. Some parents plan to stay home or tag along to meet your date in order to take pictures. You may think they are being silly until you look at the photos a few weeks (or maybe even a few

> **UMBRELLA**
>
> **Picture this:** You are driving over to your date's house to pick her up. A drop of rain hits the windshield, followed by a few more. By the time you get to her house it's a bit of a drizzle. And as she comes to the door in her gorgeous gown, it starts to pour. But you are the suave one. You have thought ahead. You produce an umbrella and say, "Please, let me keep you dry." Now that is a move she'll never forget!

years) after the prom to remind you of the night.

Be prepared to spend some time taking pictures. You'll want a variety of pictures taken with different combinations of people. With digital cameras you can take as many as you want and share the whole batch with everyone. Think ahead about what photos you know you'll want:

- You alone
- You with your date
- Your date alone
- Head shots
- Full body shots
- The whole group with whom you are going (if that's the case)
- Indoors and/or outdoors scenes
- Some candid shots throughout the night

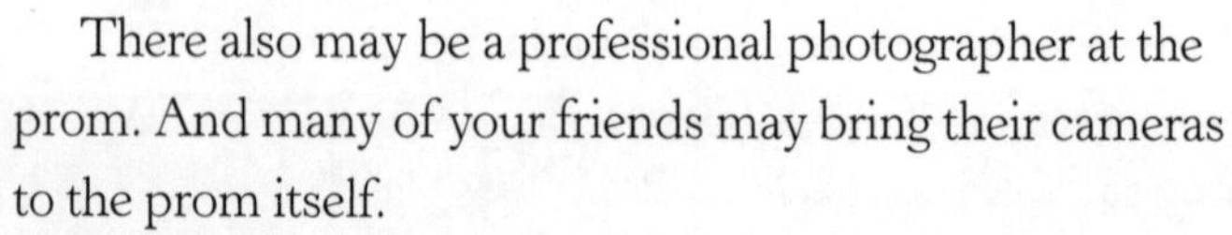

There also may be a professional photographer at the prom. And many of your friends may bring their cameras to the prom itself.

AT THE PROM . . .

Tickets, Please!

When you arrive at the prom, you may need to wait in line at the entrance, where someone from the prom committee and an adult chaperone will be taking tickets.

Line manners are no different just because you are dressed in a tuxedo or a gown. Use the time to greet those around you, talk with your friends who are in line with you, and just relax. Take a deep breath, switch slowly to your party mode, and enjoy this evening you've been looking forward to for so long!

Cell Phones

A QUESTION FOR CINDY AND PEGGY

***QUESTION:* Is it okay to talk or text on your cell phone at the prom?**

ANSWER: *The most considerate and respectful thing is to pay attention to the people you are with. Turn the question around. How would you feel if your date spent her time texting her friend who didn't go to the prom? You've spent a small fortune on tickets, dinner, flowers, a limo, and renting a tuxedo and she spends the evening on the phone with her friend. In a survey of teens who went to a prom, 71 percent responded with a straight no to this question. A quick call to verify transportation or discuss a change in plans is fine, but talking and texting in a social manner is* not *okay!*

May I Have This Dance?

Is it okay to slow dance with someone other than your date? The teens in a survey conducted by The Emily Post Institute were split sixty-forty in response to this question. Sixty percent responded that it was okay to slow dance with someone other than your date, and 40 percent thought that would not be okay.

On the other hand, 95 percent thought it was fine to fast dance with someone other than your date. The etiquette point is to be sensitive to the feelings of your date. If you think it might be hurtful, don't do it. Unless you and your date have a clear understanding, stick with your date for the more intimate dances of the evening and enjoy a dance with your other friends during the fast and less intimate dances.

It's a Social Event

Many teens describe the prom as the most significant or important evening of their high school experience. Everyone is dressed up. Oftentimes the class has chosen a theme and the space has been decorated to match the theme. Some proms have ice sculptures, some have glittering balls, some have elegant place settings, and some have props and backdrops. DJs play music. The list is endless.

This is probably not the intimate evening where you and your date have no room for anyone else. Enjoy the company of all your friends. Holding hands or putting an arm around your date can affirm the importance of being there with one special person; but don't forget to talk, laugh, and celebrate the evening with others who are there. This is an evening of shared experiences. Make the most of it.

After the Prom . . .

After the prom you might go for a late-night breakfast at a local diner. You might get together with a few friends and continue dancing at a club or an after-prom party. Maybe your friends have rented a room at the hotel in which the prom is held or maybe you simply go home. There is no one right choice for post-prom activities; but as with everything else associated with prom night, you should give it some thought ahead of time. You will probably make your plan with your date and any others with whom you are going to the prom. Since it is likely to be a late-night affair, you also will want to be clear with your parents about what you will be doing. Two seniors going to the prom together may have different parameters than a senior who is taking a freshman as a date. Before making your post-prom plans, there are some things to consider:

- If the party is at a private home, will parents be around?
- Is it an unofficial get-together without any adults?
- Will there be a keg of beer or other alcoholic beverages?
- Do you know who else is going?
- How late do you want to be out?
- If the party is at a club, will there be a limit on how many can go, and do you need a reservation?
- If you are planning an overnight at a hotel, will there be an option for a same-sex room, or will you find yourself sharing a room with members of the opposite sex?
- How will people get there?
- How will you get home?

It's your choice to make. Will you be putting yourself in a position you know is wrong for you? Will you have to lie to your parents about where you will be? Will you be putting your date in an awkward situation? You may choose to do something different. If you don't want to go to the party after the prom, make other arrangements for getting home. It may feel a little awkward, but you may find others who would be glad to join you for a ride home or for the opportunity to rehash the prom over some pizza. The best plan is one that keeps you in control of your own decisions and allows you to respect yourself and the people you are with. Use your common sense.

SOME DIFFICULT CHOICES

Here, Have a Beer. . . .

A QUESTION FOR CINDY AND PEGGY

QUESTION:* *I've made the decision not to drink alcohol. I hate the taste and I'd just rather not. What if there's a keg and lots of drinking at the after-prom party? How can I say "No, thanks" without sounding like a prude?

ANSWER: *You have to choose the tone and style of your answer. Here are some ideas:*

1. *You can always say, "No thanks, I'd rather drink a soda," and leave it at that.*
2. *Or you can say, "That's okay, I'm not really a beer drinker."*
3. *Say, "No thanks," and figure out a way to leave. Ask your date to give you a ride. Or if that isn't possible, call your parents: "I'm not really having a great time here. Could you come get me?"*

The right answer really depends on you. You need to consider the legal issues associated with underage drinking. You want to avoid being personally implicated (even if you don't drink, if you are present and bad things happen, you may be implicated). It's a big responsibility and the choice can be difficult. The important thing for you is to show respect for yourself and your friends by acting in a way that really represents who you are and what you believe.

A "Special" Act for a Special Evening?

Some teens talk about prom night as the night they might have sex for the first time because the night feels special and significant. The important thing is that you give the decision some serious thought before prom night. You don't want to make a decision you might regret while you are caught up in the emotion of this amazing evening. Ask yourself:

- Do I feel pressure to do this because everyone else is?
- Is everyone else really doing it or just talking big?
- Will I be able to look this person in the eye the next morning and talk about the experience?
- If we break up afterward anyway, how will I feel?
- Am I willing to buy and use condoms?
- Have I spoken to my partner about STDs (sexually transmitted diseases) and birth control?
- Do I really trust this person?

- Do I really love this person, and does that make a difference?
- Is this the way I want to express my love?

Sex is the most intimate act between two people, so you should take the time to consider all of these questions and answer them coolly and honestly. Most important of all, make your own decision. Don't let someone else—or the magic of prom night—cloud your judgment.

THE NEXT DAY

After you've had some breakfast the next morning, your parents will be looking forward to hearing all about the prom! Take a few minutes to talk with them. You may not realize that they have caught some of your excitement about the prom and they may be anxious to hear about the couples, the clothes, the music, the decorations, and the food. Their questions may seem endless, but talking to them about the prom will help you sort out all of your impressions and solidify the memories that are most important to you. You may want to collect your memories in a journal so you can remember prom details for many years to come.

And now it's time to touch base with your friends. So begins the "post-game" talk. The key here is to keep it from digressing into a gossip fest that could spoil the whole event. Take care not to distort things in a way that can hurt others. Focus on the positive. Revisit the humorous things that happened. Laugh and enjoy the prom all over again. As you listen to your friends' experiences, you may discover some new things to enjoy.

What is it that makes a prom so special? It is a night full of firsts and onlys. It occurs close to the end of your high school experience. It is a chance to celebrate and socialize with classmates—many of whom have been your friends for ten or more years. So enjoy! Take time to plan and make choices about your prom experience that will allow you to remember the evening and the people with whom you shared it in the best way possible.

CHAPTER FOUR

THROW YOUR HAT IN THE AIR: It's Graduation Time

Thirteen years ago, you put on your new sneakers, you packed up your crayons and pencils, and you grabbed your snack. Your mother or father drove you to your new school, or they saw you onto that huge yellow bus.

Today, you put on your new shoes, you pack up the cards you got for your friends, and you figure out how to put that crazy-looking black square cap (called a mortarboard) on your head without wrecking your hair.

So much has happened in between. There have been friends who have come and gone. There have been teachers you loved and some you didn't like too much. There have been classes that got you to think and classes you thought were boring. There have been sports teams that won and teams that lost. How can you capture all that in one celebration? That is the challenge that goes along with graduation.

The official ceremony at the school—the one in which you are handed a diploma—will have speakers and awards that help capture some of the academic accomplishments of those years. You may go to awards banquets, where sportsmanship and physical accomplishments are celebrated. If you are a member of a school club, each will have its own send-off. The spring of your senior year in high school is marked with celebrations and ceremonies that highlight all the years past and launch you into a new world.

What will your own personal graduation plans entail?

- Will you and your parents host a graduation celebration for friends and family at your home?
- Will you attend a graduation celebration at a friend's house?
- Does the school sponsor a graduation party for the entire graduation class?

Many teens will attend one, two, or all three of these events. It takes some planning and thought because you are sharing these celebrations with the people who are dearest to you: your family and your close friends. They all want some opportunity to celebrate with you. They have all contributed in different ways to your success, and it is important that you acknowledge them and allow them to share in your accomplishment.

CELEBRATE AT HOME

A QUESTION FOR CINDY AND PEGGY

QUESTION: ***My grandparents are coming to visit the weekend of my graduation. I want to do something special with them, but I also want to celebrate with my friends. What should I do?***

ANSWER: *Carve out a special celebration time that includes your grandparents. Following a morning or afternoon graduation, you and your parents can host a brunch, lunch, or dinner party. The guest list will include, of course, your grandparents.*

How Many and Who?

At this party, set aside time for your family members. The number of people you wish to invite will dictate what type of party you plan. If you have eight brothers and sisters, two nieces, four cousins, three uncles, four aunts, four grandparents, and two parents, you might have a barbecue in the backyard, where you could easily handle twenty-eight people. On the other hand, if you have two parents, one sister, two grandparents, an aunt, and one cousin, you might all go together to a local restaurant, where you would have a table for eight. It's a matter of both budget and space. You and your parents can make the final choice.

Anyone Else?

Once you've made a decision about the type of party and the place, you can begin the process of building the guest list (see Chapter One, pages 10–12). In addition to the general considerations for any guest list, there are some specifics that you need to keep in mind for a graduation party. Consider inviting:

- Immediate family members
- Cousins, aunts, and uncles
- Close family friends and neighbors
- Close friends from your class (they may be involved with their own family parties, but some seniors work

out a way to make the rounds to multiple graduation parties)

- Teachers who have had a special place in your school career (they may also have several parties to attend, so be understanding if they can come only for a short time)

Invitations

Depending on the space they have available, some schools have to put a limit on the number of people each senior can invite to the actual graduation. If you have a limited number of invitations, you need to make decisions about who you will invite to the ceremony. In addition to the invitations, you will probably be given announcement

BEGGING FOR GIFTS?

Even if the school does not place a limit on the number of invitations you can send out, you should not send invitations to people who are already included in the ceremony. Usually gifts are given by people who receive an invitation, so it might seem like you are begging for a gift by sending invitations to teachers, parents of other graduates, or family members who live far away and are not likely to attend.

On the other hand, there is no obligation to send a gift associated with receiving an announcement. People who receive an announcement *may* send a congratulatory note or card (or perhaps a small gift if they choose). So, announcements are a nice way to let people know about your accomplishment without it looking as if you're begging for a gift!

notices that you can send to everyone else. These include a place for the graduate's name or cards that can be inserted with the announcements so the recipients know which graduate sent it. There is no limit on the number of announcements you can send out.

For your family celebration, feel free to send casual, informal, or formal invitations depending on the occasion (for details about the information you should include in your invitation, see Chapter One, page 13). You can either purchase invitations or write your own note.

Dear Aunt Maria,

I am so excited to be graduating from Waterville High School on June 18. Mom and Dad are hosting an informal dinner at our house to celebrate. The festivities will begin at 5:30. I hope you can join us. Please call (878-555-1234) and let us know whether or not you can attend by June 10.

Love,

Rosaline

Whichever type of invitation you choose, include an RSVP in some form (address, phone number, or email address) so you will know how many people to expect.

Gifts

Some of your guests will want to give you a gift to help celebrate your graduation. Others might bring cards that may or may not include a check, gift card, or cash. At some point during the party you can gather everyone around and open cards and gifts. While you show the gifts and perhaps even pass them around for all to see, you should not announce the amount of money in any card. If you want to pass around the cards also, take out any checks or cash and put them aside. Even if you thank everyone right there in person, it's a good idea to also send thank-you notes—just a short note thanking each person for the gift and making a personal comment:

Dear Aunt Martha,

Thank you so much for the leather picture frame you gave me for graduation. It now holds a lovely picture of me and my friends from this year's prom. It will be just perfect in my college dorm room next semester.

It was great to see you at the graduation. I know it's quite a drive, and I'm glad you were able to do it. I'll see you at Cousin Marianne's wedding next month. I'm looking forward to it! Thanks again for the frame.

Love you,
Beth

Make it easy on yourself. Buy some colorful stationery and envelopes ahead of time and have a nice pen handy. All you need beyond the basic supplies is a list—perhaps made at the graduation party—with people's names and addresses and then a quick and easy hour to get them all done.

Once you've finished writing your notes, don't forget to mail them! It's a shame to go to all the effort and then to have them sit at the back of your desk. Before graduation, stop by the post office and pick out some special stamps or, better yet, order them online.

THANKS FOR THE CASH

A note that just says "Thanks for the cash" is boring to read and doesn't really show your appreciation. When thanking someone for a gift of money, you can write about how you plan to use it. Here are two examples:

Your check for $50 is going right into my laptop fund. I'm about halfway there. I know it will be so helpful when I get to college this fall. Thank you so much.

or

I just bought an awesome new shawl with the check you gave me for graduation. I can wear it with just about everything I have and will think about you each time I put it on. Thank you so much!

It is your choice whether or not to put the actual amount in your thank-you note. The important thing is to say thank you!

A FRIEND'S FAMILY CELEBRATION

You've gone through twelve years of school together. You do everything together. But now, on one of the most important celebrations, you'll be at your house and he'll be at his! You want that friend by your side. What to do?

Coordinate your party schedules. Maybe you can start yours a little earlier, celebrate with your family and have your friend over before his begins. Then when yours ends a little earlier than his, you can go over and celebrate with him and his family. It's not the best, but it's better than nothing.

The main thing is to be a little flexible and compromise, and everything will work out. Just talk about it so you both know what's happening. RSVP when you receive your invitation to your friend's house so his parents will know what to expect. Confirm with your friend whether or not he'll be able to join you and then let your parents know. And just like your family will want the chance to congratulate him, his family will want to congratulate you.

If you and your friend will be exchanging gifts, you can leave your gifts at each other's party or you can make the exchange at another time when you can do it in person. Either is acceptable. The most important thing to remember is that this is a time for everyone to celebrate with you. The one thing you do not want to do is end up in a little clique with your friends and ignore your relatives who may have traveled a great distance to be with you. If you are at a friend's party, the reverse is true. Be aware that he needs to spend time with his grandparents and aunts and uncles as well. Don't be a graduate hog. You'll have plenty of time later to celebrate and reminisce together.

PROJECT GRADUATION

In 1979 in Oxford Hills, Maine, seven teens were killed in alcohol-related car crashes. They had combined graduation celebrations and drinking. The community responded by creating the first Project Graduation. Parents, local business owners, and other volunteers provided students with parties that served as an alternative to graduation night drinking and driving temptations. Since then there have been Project Graduation activities in all fifty states. Parties are held at a variety of venues, including health clubs, YMCAs, and retreat centers, and on boats. Dancing, eating, sports activities, games, and prize drawings throughout the evening are part of the opportunity to celebrate and reminisce in a drug- and alcohol-free environment.

If your school provides a Project Graduation party, take advantage of it while keeping some basic etiquette standards in mind. By all means, play by the "rules." Many schools actually have contracts that students sign, agreeing to the rules established for the event. Some guidelines may include:

- NO alcohol or drugs are allowed at the party.
- Students are bused to the party from a common pickup point. Students do not bring their own cars.

- Once there you agree to stay there. You may not leave and return.
- You must show respect for the site where the party is held.
- You should treat the parents and community members who volunteer to help out with the respect they deserve.

SCHOOL CELEBRATIONS

Some schools may host a dance or celebration for the graduating class at a local hotel or ballroom. Faculty and parents volunteer to chaperone. DJs or bands provide music. The event committee arranges for the food, beverages, and decorations. All that the graduates have to do is buy tickets or sign up ahead of time so the committee can plan adequately for the event. Food, music, dancing, talking—what could be better? Your class may decide on a theme or simply go with decorations and special lighting. The options are endless. When asked what made this party a special part of their school career, teens responded that they

TWELVE YEARS! A VIDEO HISTORY

Picture this: You arrive at your school graduation party. The room is divided into three sections:

- In one, the floor has been kept clear for dancing.
- In another, tables and chairs are set up where seniors can sit with their friends to talk, laugh, and eat.
- And in the third section, there is a large screen hanging on the wall with a projector looping a slide show that highlights your whole class and your twelve years together. The slide show includes: pictures of everyone in the class at all ages, clips of events in your class history—such as that field trip you all took in eighth grade, pictures of the teachers you've known and loved through the years, various candid shots taken around the school campus.

In order for the video history to work, everyone has to pitch in and submit photos and/or videos. The yearbook staff should be able to help out with extra photographs. And someone needs to be willing to put it all together. It takes work, but the end product can be the highlight of your graduation celebration.

particularly liked the opportunity to spend time and have fun with their classmates before each of them headed off in a different direction after graduation.

CHAPTER FIVE

HOMECOMING: Show Your Spirit

What made homecoming the best day ever: enjoying high school events with friends, showing school spirit at the big game, and getting out on the dance floor at the homecoming dance party. Homecoming is a traditional event in every region of the country. At homecoming, alumni (former students of your high school), teachers, parents, and students come together to celebrate their common ground: high school. Typically, homecoming occurs in the fall and includes a sports event (most often football) that serves as the centerpiece of the weekend. During the week prior to the game, there are different activities that build school spirit; then there is the game itself; and finally, at many homecomings, there is a school dance for all the students and alumni.

SPIRIT WEEK OR SPIRIT DAY

There is a special flavor to homecoming that sets it apart from the other teen parties. Homecoming is an intergenerational event. The dance might be primarily for teens, but most of the activities are intended to be enjoyed by all ages. Taking part in these events can be an important part of high school life.

Dress-up days: Throughout the week there may be theme-related "dress-up days." For instance, mascot day, school-color day, toga or pirate day, sports hero day, or just about anything the spirit committee can imagine. These events should be silly, fun, and spirit-filled; but it's still important to keep within the boundaries that apply to any other school function. Dress-up is not a license to reveal too much, forgo cleanliness, or offend others.

After-school events: There may be special events after school all week long that celebrate the high school and provide opportunities to build spirit. For example, one day there may be a fair with exhibits that highlight the accomplishments of current and past students from the school. Another day there might be a reception for returning alumni to meet current students and staff. The chorus and band might present a music recital. Tradition may be the determining factor.

Royalty: At many schools across the country there is a homecoming king and queen selected from the senior class. Before all the homecoming festivities begin, the student body (or the class) nominates and then elects a "royal court." The king and queen preside over many of the homecoming festivities. If there is a parade, they ride in a special car. They may be crowned at a school assembly before homecoming or at the pep rally. And they appear with their court (some of those who were nominated but not elected) at the homecoming dance.

Parades: On the day of the big game, there may be a parade with floats, cars, cheerleaders, the high school band, and school officials (adults and students). There may be competitions for the best, most humorous, prettiest, or weirdest floats. Often classes or school organizations will band together to create floats.

Pep rallies: Before the big game, many schools have a rally, which might include cheerleading displays, the introduction of the homecoming king and queen (if the school has them), skits, talks by the coaches and some of the players, school songs, and, maybe a performance by the dance team. Students, staff, and alumni come together to share their excitement and to build enthusiasm about the big game to come.

The big game! Often the big game is one scheduled with the traditional crosstown rival. Alumni fans have been rooting for the home team for ten, twenty, or thirty years. The students are rooting for their friends and showing their school pride. It's an exciting day, and everyone from every generation attends!

Because homecoming combines many different generations, it's especially easy to inadvertently offend others. Building spirit and enthusiasm can lead to overexuberance. The students currently at the school have a language and style of interaction that might be unfamiliar to the alumni. The alumni might think: "When we were students here we would never be allowed to . . . !" Students do not have to adhere to the standards of the older generation, but they do have to show respect for those traditions of the past.

And in turn, the older alumni must respect the fact that things do change and the current students will have new and different traditions.

SPORTSMANSHIP

So much of homecoming is focused on "the big game." School spirit is infectious as everyone cheers the home team on—hopefully to victory. Whatever your generation, wearing school colors and school paraphernalia, belting out the school song, and cheering for your team add fun and excitement to the game.

A QUESTION FOR CINDY AND PEGGY

QUESTION:* *I was at the homecoming game with my father, my grandmother, and my two best friends. It was an exciting game against our school's toughest rival. There were three students from my school sitting just behind us. They were screaming at the refs, being obscene, and using really offensive language. They were totally out of line. It was so uncomfortable for all of us. What could we have done?

ANSWER: *This is a tough situation. If you know the students, you could try asking them to tone it down a bit. Maybe they don't realize how disruptive they're being. If you don't know them, you have to use good judgment. You don't want to start an argument. That would only make things worse. But if saying something might make the difference and you think you can keep your tone neutral, give it a try. You might be glad you did.*

Good spirit is really a function of good sportsmanship. If you consider the qualities of fair play, you will know how to act even in the heightened excitement of the homecoming game. Enjoy the game, and make sure those around you can enjoy it also.

SPORTSMANSHIP: MANNERS DURING COMPETITION (SPORTS, SPELLING BEES, DEBATES, ELECTIONS)	
On the Field of Competition	**In the Stands**
Follow the rules of the game	Follow the rules of the arena or auditorium
Don't argue with judges or referees	Don't yell or boo the judges or referees
Be considerate of the other players	Don't yell or boo the other players
Be respectful of coaches	Don't yell or boo the coaches
Thank the other team and congratulate the players on a good competition when you're done	Cheer for the winner, but remember to thank the loser and congratulate the players on a good competition

In a survey about homecoming, teens helped identify the dos and don'ts of watching the big game:

Do:

- Stand for the national anthem
- Take off your hat for the national anthem
- Dress in school colors
- Cheer as loud as you can
- Use noisemakers for cheering

Don't:

- Boo the other team
- Swear/curse during the game
- Throw items onto the field
- Belch loudly or spit
- Use noisemakers just to make noise

If you want . . .

- Wear face and body paint

Half of the respondents to our survey thought it was okay to boo at a bad call. On the other hand, half thought you shouldn't. We'd advise enjoying the game without booing or creating disruptions.

THE DANCE!

After all the spirit raising, the cheering, the parades, the face paint, the school colors, and the game itself, it's time to dance! The dance is often the high point of homecoming week. Local traditions often make the homecoming dance different from other school dances. For example, the role of the king and queen (if there is royalty) is determined by tradition. They often preside over the dance. Some schools have a traditional dance for the king and queen, but then they are free to dance with whomever they like. They may wear sashes and crowns that identify them in their special role. At some schools there is a table designated for the king and queen and their court.

At many schools the dance is decorated based on a theme selected by one of the classes, by the dance committee, or by the student body. The theme will govern the decor, the table centerpieces, and perhaps the food. If the theme is a Hawaiian one, the menu might be planned to resemble a luau.

Themes will vary from school to school. As time passes, some traditions will fade away and new ones will evolve. But the key thing is to show respect for your high school's traditions so that you can enjoy them when you become an alumnus and return for homecoming week yourself.

Music

The theme of the homecoming dance will likely dictate the type of music played. If the theme is a hoedown, the music is likely to be country and western. A big band theme might suggest an entirely different kind of music. It might not be your favorite style of music, but give it a try. Bundled together with decorations and food, you might discover you like something new.

"PLEASE PLAY MY FAVORITE SONG": THE ETIQUETTE OF MAKING A SONG REQUEST

- Go up to the DJ or band and make your request. Don't shout out your favorite songs from the dance floor.
- Use a request sheet if one is made available.
- If there is a line, wait your turn. Let others get their requests in also.
- Ask for a specific song and artist and let the DJ find it unless there is a book or list displayed. Don't ask to look through a DJ's albums yourself.
- Approach the band when the members are between songs, not while they are playing.
- If the DJ doesn't have your song or the band doesn't know it, say "Thanks anyway" and get back on the dance floor.

The choice to hire a band or a DJ can be driven either by budget or theme. Typically, bands are more expensive unless the committee selects a band from within the student body. The band may be limited to one style of music, so for many dances a DJ is a good choice. In any case, a good sound system, colorful lighting, and a large dance floor will all contribute to a great event.

GO, TEAM, GO

The whole point of homecoming is to create a sense of community and school spirit for everyone who attends. It is everyone's responsibility to be welcoming to alumni and to support the homecoming week activities. Enjoy the alumni. Take time to listen to their stories and tell them your own. In years to come when you meet someone who graduated from your high school, there will always be a special bond. Make the most of homecoming, and help others around you enjoy it also.

CHAPTER SIX

ACT YOUR AGE: Coming-of-Age Celebrations

The teen years mark a major transitional period in every young person's life. During these years you move from being a child to being a young adult. It is an exciting journey filled with new adventures and emotional events. Throughout your teen years you will be exposed to a variety of events that celebrate these transitions. Some are based on religious milestones (bar/bat mitzvah, confirmation), some on the passage of time (quinceañera, sweet sixteen birthday), and some on tradition (cotillions or debutante balls).

Each category of coming-of-age party is unique. Some parties are driven by culture and some are driven by tradition. What will you need to know in order to add to and enjoy each celebration? In this chapter we'll review the answers to the following questions:

- What should I wear?

- Can I bring a date?
- Will there be food?
- Can I expect to dance?
- Should I bring a gift?

CINDY AND PEGGY'S TOP FIVE SUGGESTIONS FOR STRESS-FREE GIFT GIVING

1. Ask the recipient for hints or a wish list.
2. Trust your judgment. Forget about being afraid that the gift may not be perfect. If you think it's just right, it probably is!
3. Stick to your budget. Spending more than you should takes the fun out of it.
4. Buy it when you see it. If you know your best friend is having a sweet sixteen party this year and you see the perfect gift a few months before, buy it. It may not be there later.
5. Keep a few gifts stashed away in your closet. You may be going to several coming-of-age parties, and you'll want to bring a gift. If you plan ahead and keep a few nice gifts on hand, you can save time and avoid stress before the actual event.

WHAT DO I DO DURING A TRADITIONAL ACTIVITY THAT IS UNFAMILIAR TO ME?

These questions come up over and over again. Knowing what to do and how to plan will give you the confidence to attend new events and feel comfortable. After all, that is what etiquette can do for you: allow you to know what to expect from others and what others may expect of you. It really is that simple, so let's look at some specific coming-of-age parties and see what's up!

RELIGIOUS COMING-OF-AGE CELEBRATIONS

Confirmations and Bar and Bat Mitzvahs

Both of these ceremonies are grounded in religious traditions. The teen being celebrated has studied hard and attended classes, and emerges from the experience ready to be a participating adult member of the congregation. Confirmation occurs in the Christian tradition, and while it is a coming-of-age event, it is not usually celebrated with a big party for classmates and other teens. If you are invited to a friend's confirmation mass and are not familiar with the church, ask what you should wear. Semiformal or festive attire is a good bet. After the confirmation at the church, there may be a reception with beverages, snacks, and sometimes a cake for family, friends, and members of the congregation. Family and close friends may bring small gifts, but this is not an expectation. In addition, the family may host a lunch or small celebration at their home.

A bar mitzvah is the coming-of-age ceremony for Jewish boys, which is traditionally celebrated when they are thirteen—sometimes a little older. A bat mitzvah is the coming-of-age ceremony for Jewish girls. The bat mitzvah is held when a girl is twelve or thirteen. After the religious ceremony, there is often a gathering at the synagogue that is open to any member of the congregation who wishes to offer congratulations.

Later in the day, the family may host a luncheon or dinner at their home or at a restaurant, club, or hotel. Some of these "invitation only" celebrations can be quite simple; some can be extravagant. There may or may not be a band with dancing and singing as part of the festivities. Family,

members of the congregation, friends, and classmates may be on the guest list. If you have a close Jewish friend, you are likely to be invited to the bar or bat mitzvah.

What should I wear? For many bar and bat mitzvahs the dress is semiformal (see Chapter One, page 19). Unless the invitation indicates "formal" or "black tie," girls can wear dresses or dressy long or short skirts, and boys can wear suits or dark jackets and slacks. If there is a luncheon following the service, then guests can wear the clothes they wore to the ceremony.

Do I bring a date? No. Only those who receive an invitation should attend.

Will there be food? Yes, and probably lots of food, so do not eat a big meal before going.

Can I expect to dance? There will most likely be dancing and perhaps some traditional Jewish dancing. There may be some singing also. If you don't know the song or the dance, just listen, join in when you get the hang of it, clap, and enjoy!

Should I bring a gift? All guests are expected to bring a gift just as you would to a birthday party. It doesn't have to be extravagant: a book, a gift certificate, a CD, jewelry, or something you know your friend would enjoy. Be sure to include a card, as your friend may not open gifts at the reception and you will want to be sure she knows what you

WHEN GOING TO ANY UNFAMILIAR RELIGIOUS SERVICE

Things to ask your host:

- What do I wear?
- What can I expect?
- Is there anything special I need to do or not do?

picked out for her.

What do I do during a traditional activity that is unfamiliar to me? For the most part, simply watch those around you and follow their lead. No one will expect you to sing, dance, or participate in any religious blessings or prayers; but you can follow their lead. If you go to the religious service, stay alert and keep pace with the congregation as they stand or sit. Boys should be prepared to wear a yarmulke at almost all synagogues. Some reform synagogues may not require it, but those that do will provide them at the entrance to the synagogue.

Confirmations and bar and bat mitzvahs are great ways to celebrate your friends in their early teen years. Even if the religious customs are unfamiliar, enjoy yourself and take the opportunity to learn a little more about a different tradition.

Quinceañera

Quince is the Spanish word for *fifteen*, and that is what this party is all about. The quinceañera (or quince, as it is often called) is a traditional celebration of a girl's fifteenth birthday. The event marks her "transition" from girlhood to womanhood. There is a religious element (usually a special Mass) that is grounded in the Roman Catholic church and a festive celebration that follows. Some families do not participate in the religious ceremony but do have a party for their daughter. In either case, the fifteen-year-old girl is the honoree, and the family is celebrating her coming-of-age.

QUINCEAÑERA, DON'T BE CONFUSED!

Both the party and the girl being honored are referred to as the "quinceañera."

There are many aspects to the traditional quince. The customs and traditions may differ depending on the family's country of origin, and some girls and their families place different levels of importance on different traditions. However, there are some elements that occur at every quinceañera. For instance, the girl's dress is always formal. Usually it is a white, full-skirted, floor-length gown. The members of her "court," made up of young girls (*damas*) and young men (*chambelanes*), also dress formally in gowns and tuxedos. If you have had your own quince or have been to others, you will have some idea what to expect. If you have not, just know that you can expect an event filled with music, food, dancing, emotions, laughter, and tears.

What do I wear? The guests at a quince should wear formal or semiformal clothes.

Do I bring a date? Unless the invitation specifically states that you can bring a guest, you should not. The food and space is planned for a set number of guests, and it is not your choice to increase that number.

Will there be food? Yes. You should not eat a big dinner before you go.

Can I expect to dance? Yes. There will be some celebratory dances: The quinceañera may dance with her father in front of everyone, and there will be set dances that the quinceañera and her court do as everyone watches. When they are finished, everyone dances.

Should I bring a gift? Unless the invitation says "No gifts, please," you should bring a gift, just as you would to any birthday party.

What do I do during a traditional activity that is unfamiliar to me? As with every new situation, just watch those around you and follow suit. If there is something happening and you are curious about its meaning, ask someone who seems to know. Either you will find someone else who is curious or you will learn something new.

Throughout the party there are traditional events that mark the passage from *niña* to *senorita*. All of these activities do not happen at every quinceañera, but it is fun to see the ones that do.

- The quinceañera's court, made up of male and female escorts called *chambelanes* and *damas*, wears formal clothes that are often coordinated both in color and style.
- Choreographed entrance and dance performance by the court take place as the emcee announces the entrance of the parents, brothers and sisters, and court. The *chambelanes* and *damas* enter the room, bow to each other, and perform a choreographed routine. The guests all watch and applaud.
- The quinceañera enters in her beautiful princesslike dress. Everyone applauds!
- She wears a tiara that is a symbol of leaving childhood behind and facing the challenges that come with adulthood. 
- She changes from flat shoes to high heels, which also symbolizes the transition to adulthood.
- She wears a gift of a bracelet or ring that symbolizes the unending circle of life.
- She wears earrings as a reminder to listen to the word

of God and to hear and respond to the world that surrounds her.

- She carries a Bible, cross, rosary, prayer book, or medallion, any of which signify her faith in God and in her world.
- The quinceañera may dance a special dance with her father as all her family and guests watch and applaud.
- The quinceañera may light a candle for each of the important people in her life. She may give a little speech that honors each person as he or she comes forward to stand by her. A final candle is lit for someone who is special but not able to be there.

NONRELIGIOUS RITES OF PASSAGE

Cotillion or Debutante Party

While a debutante ball is no longer a festivity in which a young woman is "presented to society," it remains a celebration of a young woman's coming-of-age. The celebrations and rituals vary from place to place; but generally speaking, most debutante balls will look similar, though the party may vary in size. The most elaborate type of party is the private ball. It may be given by an individual's family or by the families of several debutantes together. Sometimes the party is put on by an organization that invites a group of girls to participate. These events are often done as a benefit, and the party's proceeds are given to various charities. Whatever form the debutante ball takes, the girls will attend with their parents, close families, one or two escorts, and a limited number of guests. The debutante ball or cotillion is not a gathering of the girl's entire high school class. If you are invited to be a guest of a debutante, you will probably be seated with a group of her friends. It will be a very different experience from the school dance or prom.

What do I wear? This is usually a formal event. The female guests wear evening gowns of any color except white (the debutantes wear white) or black. The guys wear tuxedos (black tie).

Do I bring a date? No. The number of guests is set by the host family or group, and unless the invitation indicates that you may bring a guest, don't.

Will there be food? Usually at a debutante ball dinner is served, so do not eat a large meal before going.

Can I expect to dance? Yes. After the debutante has a

dance with her father and her escort(s), everyone dances.

Should I bring a gift? No. This is not like a birthday party. Relatives and close friends may send gifts, but this isn't required. If you are an escort, you may send flowers and give the debutante a corsage. Check with her beforehand to see if she plans to wear a corsage.

What do I do during a traditional activity that is unfamiliar to me? Your role as a guest is to observe. There may be traditional cotillion dances, but only the debutante and her father participate in those. The debutante is the one who will be "presented" and who may have to be part of a receiving line or curtsy to the committee. The guests simply need to go through the line. In 1922, Emily Post gave this advice for the guest:

> *Each arriving guest always shakes hands with the debutante as well as with the hostess, and if there is a queue of people coming at the same time, there is no need of saying anything beyond "How do you do?" and passing on as quickly as possible. If there are no others entering at the moment, each guest makes a few pleasant remarks. A stranger, for instance, would perhaps comment on how lovely, and many, the debutante's bouquets are, or express a hope that she will enjoy her winter, or talk for a moment or two about the "gaiety of*

> *the season" or "the lack of balls," or anything that shows polite interest in the young girl's first glimpse of society. A friend of her mother might perhaps say "You look too lovely, Cynthia dear, and your dress is enchanting!" Personal compliments, however, are proper only from a close friend. No acquaintance, unless she is quite old, should ever make personal remarks. An old lady or gentleman might very forgivably say "You don't mind, my dear, if I tell you how sweet I think you look," or "What a pretty frock you have on." But it is bad taste for a young woman to say to another "What a handsome dress you have on!" and worst of all to add "Where did you get it?" The young girl's particular friends are, of course, apt to tell her that her dress is wonderful, or more likely, "simply divine."*

Guests are guests the world around and from age to age. The specifics of what you say may change, but generally something pleasant and congratulatory works perfectly and will help to set the evening off on a great path.

Happy Birthday to You!

For some teens turning sixteen means freedom—the freedom that comes with a driver's license. For others turning sixteen brings a special party that celebrates coming-of-age.

Whether it's a small gathering of family and friends or a big blowout party at a local club, a sweet sixteen party is a special rite of passage. As a guest, it is important for you to be aware of the traditions so you can plan accordingly.

What do I wear? The invitation should definitely tell you how to dress: formal, semiformal, or casual. If the party has a theme, you might be asked to dress accordingly. In any case, a good guest makes the effort to dress in the style indicated.

Do I bring a date? Unless the invitation specifies that you can bring a guest, you should not bring one.

Will there be food? The invitation usually indicates whether or not there will be dinner, such as "Come to a barbecue celebrating my sixteenth birthday."

Or you can determine if a meal will be served based on the time of the party. At a party from 5:30 to 8:00 you can expect that dinner will be served. At a party that starts at 8:00 there will probably be no dinner, just snacks and beverages.

Can I expect to dance? The invitation may or may not answer this question. Even if it says nothing about dancing, there still may be music, and some of the guests may begin dancing. You can choose to join if you want.

Should I bring a gift? Yes, this is a birthday party! However, if the invitation states "No gifts, please," bringing one would put everyone on the spot. The birthday girl might feel awkward, and the other guests might feel as if they had missed a clue somewhere. If you want to give her a gift, do so at another time.

GIFT IDEAS FOR A SWEET SIXTEEN PARTY

- A charm for a charm bracelet
- Jewelry
- Any book on her special interest or hobby
- Personalized stationery
- Scarf, belt, or other fashion accessory

What do I do during a traditional activity that is unfamiliar to me? There may be a family tradition that is not familiar to you. The invitation is not likely to indicate that. The simplest thing to do if you find yourself in the midst of an unfamiliar custom is to watch and follow. It's also okay to ask if you are confused. It's how you ask, not that you ask, that matters: "I've never played this particular game; could you please let me know what I need to do?"

Ask, ask, ask! If the invitation only states date, time,

place, and occasion and you have questions that are unanswered, ask. It is far easier to ask questions than to show up in a formal dress when everyone else arrives in blue jeans and a T-shirt. Most party invitations come with plenty of time for you to find out the information that will help you be completely comfortable at your friend's special celebration.

WHEN WILL THE INVITATION COME?

I want to go to the party, but I have a trip with my family coming up. I want to get the date on my calendar and plan ahead. How much advance notice can I expect?

Bar or bat mitzvah—1 month
Debutante ball—6 weeks to 3 months
Graduation party—3 weeks
Quinceañera—1 month
Sweet sixteen—3 to 6 weeks

Chapter Seven

DANCE PARTY!

It can be a long haul from homecoming to the prom. Or maybe you don't have a homecoming dance, in which case it can be a long haul until graduation. The solution: a special school dance sometime in January or February, where you can shake off the winter blues!

SO IT'S NOT A PROM?

School dances share some similarities with a prom: They're sponsored by the school; they may include special clothing, themes, dinner out, and a royal court. But these dances are not the prom, nor do they take the place of the prom. Here are some basic differences:

- The prom is almost always formal; these dances may be formal but more often they are semiformal, casual, or costumed.
- Students or their parents are more apt to drive to

school dances, whereas limos are used for the prom.

- The prom is for juniors and/or seniors (with an occasional freshman or sophomore as a date). These other school dances are usually for students in grades nine to twelve.

VALENTINE'S DAY

Valentine's Day is a time to celebrate love. It also marks a time to celebrate friendship and all the people we care about in our lives. You can send flowers, cards, or candy to friends and loved ones—or maybe even to that special someone. A Valentine's Day event can be a perfect opportunity to dance with your crush or just have fun with friends.

WINTER BALL

For those in the North, celebrating winter makes a lot more sense than complaining about it. Days are short and nights are long, so why not have a dance to brighten up the evening. Snowflakes, icicles, and cool blue skies make a lovely backdrop for a beautiful winter ball. In some communities and schools, the winter ball is more than a dance. Winter activities such as skating, sledding, and skiing happen throughout the weekend or week preceding the dance. Some schools have an ice sculpture or snowman contest. And some communities even take it another step further and build an ice castle. Winter carnivals and winter balls are the best ways to enjoy the season.

SPRING FLING

The trees are budding, winter is over, the tops are down on the convertibles, and it's a special time of year. What better way to celebrate than with a dance for all the students at your school? The decorations may include pastel colors and feature flowers, the music might be upbeat and fun to usher in the new season, and the food can be fresh. Whether it's casual or semiformal, everyone can wear something that's colorful and bright. The Spring Fling is an opportunity to get together and have fun with friends on a magical spring evening.

SADIE HAWKINS DANCE

Times have changed and there is nothing unusual about girls asking boys to a dance, but a Sadie Hawkins dance sheds a special light on an old tradition. Sadie Hawkins was a character in the old *Li'l Abner* comic strip that celebrated life in Dogpatch. In the comic strip, Sadie Hawkins Day was when the unmarried women of Dogpatch chased the bachelors and each woman married the man she caught. The dance event doesn't take it that far, but years ago the tradition of the Sadie Hawkins dance was started to give girls the chance to ask guys to the dance. The practice continues even today, and Sadie Hawkins dances are still popular in some high schools.

SPECIAL-THEME DANCES

Some schools may choose to have different theme dances from year to year. One year it might be a 70s disco party with lots of polyester and feathered hairdos. Another year it might be a red-carpet theme where everyone comes dressed as a celebrity. The idea is to get together with school friends and have fun!

WHEN YOU GO TO A SCHOOL DANCE . . .

Different schools have different traditions to combat the midwinter blues. But there are some similarities. You can ask the same questions that you asked for the coming-of-age celebrations. Keep in mind that all the coming-of-age celebrations occurred outside of school, and these special dances happen at the school or are sponsored by the school and are subject to school policies.

What do I wear? One big difference between these dances and the prom is that they are less likely to be formal. The fliers for the dance should state the type of dress. It really depends on the kind of dance and possibly on the theme. For a Valentine's Day dance, the style of dress might be semiformal. Or the dance committee may specify casual dress or ask everyone to come in costumes. There is no single standard.

Do I bring a date? It's your choice. For most school dances you can come solo, with one other person as a couple, or with a group of friends. Unless it's a Sadie Hawkins dance where the whole point is for girls ask boys, it's completely okay for either a girl or a boy to ask someone special to be the date.

Will there be food? There will probably be food. The

DO I HAVE TO DANCE?

There is no rule that says you have to dance. You may prefer to go, enjoy the music, and hang out with your friends. If you feel a little shy about dancing, practice at home with your sister, your brother, or a good friend. Practice in front of the mirror. The more you practice, the more comfortable you'll feel. You may discover that you enjoy the dance more if you get out on the dance floor!

type depends on the dance. If dinner will be served, the price of the dinner will be included in the price of the ticket. The dinner will be either buffet style or served by the staff (see Chapter Two, pages 42–43 for more about buffets and banquet-style dinners).

What type of music can I expect? The dance committee will chose either a DJ or a band. Sometimes a band from the student body will perform at a school dance.

THANKS TO ALL!

Whether it's a winter ball, a Valentine's Day dance, or a theme dance for springtime, it takes many people to pull it off. Don't forget to thank them. You can thank the chaperones as you leave. They have volunteered their time, so let them know you appreciate it. Send a note to the committee members (or at least to the chair) the next day and tell them what you liked best about the dance. They spent hours organizing. A little feedback is a great pat on the back.

Dear Portia,

The Winter Ball last night was awesome. I really liked the band. They were great! They got everyone up and dancing. Thanks so much for all the time you and the other committee members spent planning. It really showed! Please share this with the others at your next meeting.

See you around—

Heather

How long can it take? Just a few minutes, and you can make a huge difference for someone else. Enjoy the dance and then help someone else feel really good about it. That doubles the pleasure!

CHAPTER EIGHT

A FINAL WORD FROM TEENS

In order to write this book, we talked to teens to see what they had to say about party etiquette. Through a combination of focus groups and surveys, we got feedback from one hundred teens across the country. We wanted to share what we learned from teens like you. Their responses informed some of the advice in this book. For instance:

- Do teens still wear formal clothes to the prom?
- We know that many things are more casual today than in the past. Is that also true of teen parties?
- Do teens still ride to the prom in limos? Do they ride in limos to any other parties?

- Is it okay to slow dance with someone other than your date?
- What do teens think of public displays of affection at school dances?
- We know the etiquette about cell phone use at the dance, but what do teens think?

DRESS UP OR DRESS DOWN?

Teens tell us that there is no question they still dress up for proms. Ninety-one percent of the teens who responded to this question on our survey dressed formally for the prom. If you go to a quinceañera, you are likely to dress formally—about 64 percent did. However, at other teen parties most teens dressed either in semiformal clothes or went casual. Several teens even told us they wore costumes or unusual, colorful clothes because of a dare or simply for fun. For homecoming and other special dances at school, semiformal dress was the standard. For parties held at home, the most frequent response was "dressy" casual or simply casual.

GETTING THERE!

Most teens drive to the prom in their own car or ride in their date's car.

Not too many walk. For a few, a sibling might have taken them or they went on public transportation. Thirty-two percent hired a limo for the prom, but only 14 percent also used a limo to go to the homecoming dance. It was interesting that parents accounted for almost as many rides as limos!

GRAB YOUR ENTOURAGE

Today you can go to the dance with a date, with your friend, or with a group of friends. This is clearly one of the areas where things have changed over time. In our conversations with teens we did not hear about boys going with a group of guys, but we do know that sometimes two or three guys might travel to the prom together if they don't have dates.

In both the surveys and the focus groups, teens talked to us about going to dances together in groups. The groups could be made up of couples, singles, or couples and singles together. What this tells us is that the important thing is no longer that you go to the dance only as a couple (although 32 percent still described their experience as a date) but that all the students have the opportunity to attend in a variety of combinations.

EXTENDING THE INVITATION

Did you have the courage to ask your date to the dance? Did you wait to get asked? The responses to this question were all over the place. For proms, it appears the date asked you; but for graduation parties, you asked your date. For homecoming, your date asked you; and for all other school dances, you asked your date. A small percentage went solo and didn't have to deal with the "ask" issue.

IT'S ALL ABOUT RELATIONSHIPS: PDA

The majority of teens thought it's perfectly fine to hold hands, hug, and kiss on the cheek; and a quick kiss on the lips is okay, too. But hardly anyone wanted to witness a heavy make-out session at the prom or any other celebration. So, lesson learned: It's best to make private, NOT public, displays of affection.

DANCE PARTNER DILEMA

Apparently, there is a strong sense that dancing and talking with others is in no way a betrayal of a relationship—at least when it happens at a public event such as a dance or a party. We congratulate this position and think it shows a maturity and a sense of trust. However, slow dancing with someone else's date was not quite as acceptable.

A BRIEF NOTE ON DANCING STYLES

When we talk about etiquette, we often ask people to consider whether their action—whatever it may be—could be offensive to others. Are there some dances that might offend? In the Roaring Twenties some people were offended by the Charleston. In the fifties, it was the lindy or the hop. In the sixties, the twist was popular but some folks found it offensive. Today, the question might be "To grind or not to grind?" Some people definitely might be offended, so we decided to ask the teens.

The responses split differently depending on the event. About half of those responding felt it was either okay or not okay to grind at either the prom, homecoming, a sweet sixteen party, or someone's quinceañera. However, they felt quite strongly that you should not grind at a graduation dance. On the other hand, it was definitely okay at other—less formal—school dances. Teens did not seem to think that grinding would be offensive to others attending the dance and generally acknowledged that it was okay.

We would only add that you consider your audience when dancing. If there are children or older people around, you should probably avoid provocative dancing of any kind regardless of the occasion.

CELL ETIQUETTE

We receive many questions these days about the use of cell phones—both texting and talking: Is it okay in this situation or that situation? As such, we decided to ask teens what they thought about it at parties and dances.

For some reason it appears to be okay at homecoming, but at any other event (except other school dances, which had a 50/50 split!), the majority of teens would rather people put away their cell phones.

SO NOW YOU'VE HEARD SOME TEENS TALKING!

The teens we heard from were thoughtful, considerate, and respectful—all the attributes we know lead to good relationships and great times. For decades proms, school dances, and other milestone events have been central to high school and the teen years. With all of the changes in each generation, it is awesome that these parties are still the highlight of teen life. It seems good food, good music, dancing, talking, and dressing up never go out of style!

A FINAL WORD . . .

We've planned and written this book with one main goal in mind: to give you some tips to help you feel more at ease at the parties you attend during your teen years. By answering the questions that come up again and again, we hope we've cut back on those moments when you're not sure what to do. Rather than being anxious, you can focus on savoring the anticipation that precedes the party, enjoying the party to the fullest, and creating great memories to cherish for years to come. The fun will then be extended beyond the event itself—to the days and weeks *before* when you're caught up in the planning and the days and weeks *after* when you reflect on the special moments.

These tips and our advice are only to enhance the celebrations and special parties you attend and are not what the party is *really* about. But it seems all of you already know that a party is much more than etiquette. The teens who sent in comments were unanimous: The best thing about any party is being with friends—dancing, talking, laughing, and celebrating these amazing years together. Now that's what a party is all about!

INDEX